# COLLECTED WRITINGS OF CHAIRMAN MAO

## VOLUME 2

# GUERRILLA WARFARE

### By

### Mao Zedong

El Paso Norte Press
Special Edition Books

Collected Writings of Chairman Mao – Volume 2
Guerrilla Warfare

By Mao Zedong

Edited by Shawn Conners

Translation of "On Guerrilla Warfare" by Samuel B. Griffith in
Fleet Marine Force Reference Publication (FMFRP) 12-18,
1989

Additional translation by Foreign Language Press, Peking


First Edition – November 2009




Published by
EL Paso Norte Press
El Paso, Texas USA

ISBN10  1-934255-26-2
ISBN13  978-1-934255-26-1


Printed in the United States of America

# CONTENTS

# COLLECTED WRITINGS OF CHAIRMAN MAO: VOLUME 2 GUERRILLA WARFARE

**Part 2:**
**Problems of Strategy in Guerrilla War against Japan**

*Mao Zedong*

**Part 3:**
**On Protracted War**

*Mao Zedong*

# COLLECTED WRITINGS OF CHAIRMAN MAO

## VOLUME 2

# GUERRILLA WARFARE

## PART 1

# ON GUERRILLA WARFARE

*Mao Zedong*

# CHAPTER I

# What Is Guerrilla Warfare?

In a war of revolutionary character, guerrilla operations are a necessary part. This is particularly true in war waged for the emancipation of a people who inhabit a vast nation. China is such a nation, a nation whose techniques are undeveloped and whose communications are poor. She finds herself confronted with a strong and victorious Japanese imperialism. Under these circumstances, the development of the type of guerrilla warfare characterized by the quality of mass is both necessary and natural. This warfare must be developed to an unprecedented degree and it must co-ordinate with the operations of our regular armies. If we fail to do this, we will find it difficult to defeat the enemy.

These guerrilla operations must not be considered as an independent form of warfare. They are but one step in the total war, one aspect of the revolutionary struggle. They are the inevitable result of the clash between oppressor and oppressed, when the latter reach the limits of their endurance. In our case, these hostilities began at a time when the people were unable to endure any more from the Japanese imperialists. Lenin, in *People and Revolution* said: "*A people's insurrection and a people's revolution are not only natural but inevitable.*" We consider guerrilla operations as but one aspect of our total or mass war because they, lacking the quality of independence, are of themselves incapable of providing a solution to the struggle.

Guerrilla warfare has qualities and objectives peculiar to itself. It is a weapon that a nation inferior in arms and military equipment may employ against a more powerful aggressor nation. When the invader pierces deep into the heart of the weaker country and occupies her territory in a cruel and oppressive manner, there is no doubt that conditions of terrain, climate, and society in general offer obstacles to his progress and may be used to advantage by those who oppose him. In guerrilla warfare we turn these advantages to the purpose of resisting and defeating the enemy.

During the progress of hostilities, guerrillas gradually develop into orthodox forces that operate in conjunction with other units of the regular army. Thus the regularly organized troops, those guerrillas who have attained that status, and those who have not reached that level of development combine to form the military power of a national revolutionary war. There can be no doubt that the ultimate result of this will be victory.

Both in its development and in its method of application, guerrilla warfare has certain distinctive characteristics. We first will discuss the relationship of guerrilla warfare to national policy. Because ours is the resistance of a semi colonial country against imperialism, our hostilities must have a clearly defined political goal and firmly established political responsibilities. Our basic policy is the creation of a national united anti-Japanese front. This policy we pursue in order to gain our political goal, which is the complete emancipation of the Chinese people. There are certain fundamental steps necessary in the realization of this policy, to wit:

1. Arousing and organizing the people.
2. Achieving internal unification politically.
3. Establishing bases.
4. Equipping forces.
5. Recovering national strength.

6. Destroying enemy's national strength.
7. Regaining lost territories.

There is no reason to consider guerrilla warfare separately from national policy. On the contrary, it must be organized and conducted in complete accord with national anti-Japanese policy. It is only those who misinterpret guerrilla action who say, as does Jen Ch'i Shan, "*The question of guerrilla hostilities is purely a military matter and not a political one.*" Those who maintain this simple point of view have lost sight of the political goal and the political effects of guerrilla action. Such a simple point of view will cause the people to lose confidence and will result in our defeat.

What is the relationship of guerrilla warfare to the people? Without a political goal, guerrilla warfare must fail, as it must, if its political objectives do not coincide with the aspirations of the people and their sympathy, co-operation, and assistance cannot be gained. The essence of guerrilla warfare is thus revolutionary in character. On the other hand, in a war of counter-revolutionary nature, there is no place for guerrilla hostilities. Because guerrilla warfare basically derives from the masses and is supported by them, it can neither exist nor flourish if it separates itself from their sympathies and co-operation. There are those who do not comprehend guerrilla action, and who therefore do not understand the distinguishing qualities of a people's guerrilla war, who say: 'Only regular troops can carry on guerrilla operations.' There are others who, because they do not believe in the ultimate success of guerilla action, mistakenly say: 'Guerrilla warfare is an insignificant and highly specialized type of operation in which there is no place for the masses of the people' (Jen Ch'i Shan). Then there are those who ridicule the masses and undermine resistance by wildly asserting that the people have no understanding of the war of resistance (Yeh Ch'ing, for one). The moment that this war of resistance dissociates itself from the masses of the people is the precise moment that it dissociates itself from hope of ultimate victory over the Japanese.

What is the organization for guerrilla warfare? Though all guerrilla bands that spring from the masses of the people suffer from lack of organization at the time of their formation, they all have in common a basic quality that makes organization possible. All guerrilla units must have political and military leadership. This is true regardless of the source or size of such units. Such units may originate locally, in the masses of the people; they may be formed from an admixture of regular troops with groups of the people, or they may consist of regular army units intact. And mere quantity does not affect this matter. Such units may consist of a squad of a few men, a battalion of several hundred men, or a regiment of several thousand men.

All these must have leaders who are unyielding in their policies—resolute, loyal, sincere, and robust. These men must be well-educated in revolutionary technique, self confident, able to establish severe discipline, and able to cope with counter-propaganda. In short, these leaders must be models for the people. As the war progresses, such leaders lack of discipline which at first will gradually overcome the lack of discipline which at first prevails; they will establish discipline in their forces, strengthening them and increasing their combat efficiency. Thus eventual victory will be attained.

Unorganized guerrilla warfare cannot contribute to victory and those who attack the movement as a combination of banditry and anarchism do not understand the nature of guerrilla action. They say, 'This movement is a haven for disappointed militarists, vagabonds, and bandits' (Jen Ch'i Shan), hoping thus to bring the movement into disrepute. We do not deny that there are corrupt guerrillas, nor that there are people who under the guise of guerrillas indulge in unlawful activities. Neither do we deny that the movement has at the present time symptoms of a lack of organization, symptoms that might indeed be serious were we to judge guerrilla warfare solely by the corrupt and temporary phenomena we have mentioned. We should study the corrupt phenomena and attempt to eradicate them in order to encourage guerilla warfare, and to increase its military efficiency. 'This is hard work, there is no help for it, and the problem cannot be solved immediately. The whole people must try to reform themselves during the course of the war. We must educate them and reform them in the light of past experience. *"Evil does not exist in guerrilla warfare but only in the unorganized and undisciplined activities that are anarchism,"* said Lenin.

What is basic guerrilla strategy? Guerrilla strategy must be based primarily on alertness, mobility, and attack. It must be adjusted to the enemy situation, the terrain, the existing lines of communication, the relative strengths, the weather and the situation of the people.

In guerrilla warfare, select the tactic of seeming to come from the east and attacking from the west; avoid the solid, attack the hollow; attack; withdraw; deliver a lightning blow, seek a lightning decision. When guerrillas engage a stronger enemy, they withdraw when he advances; harass him when he stops; strike him when he is weary; pursue him when he withdraws. In guerilla strategy, the enemy's rear, flanks, and other vulnerable spots are his vital points, and there he must be harassed, attacked, dispersed, exhausted and annihilated. Only in this way can guerrillas carry out their mission of independent guerrilla action and coordination with the effort of the regular armies. But, in spite of the most complete preparation, there can be no victory if mistakes are made in the matter of command. Guerilla warfare based on the principles we have mentioned and carried out over a vast extent of territory in which communications are inconvenient will contribute tremendously towards ultimate defeat of the Japanese and consequent emancipation of the Chinese people.

A careful distinction must be made between two types of guerrilla warfare. The fact that revolutionary guerrilla warfare is based on the masses of the people does not in itself mean that the organization of guerrilla units is impossible in a war of counter-revolutionary character. As examples of the former type we may cite Red guerilla hostilities during the Russian Revolution; those of the Reds China; of the Abyssinians against the Italians for the past three years; those of the last seven years in Manchuria, and the vast anti-Japanese guerrilla war that is carried on in China today. All these struggles have been carried on in the interest of the whole people or the greater part of them; all had a broad basis in the national manpower and all have been in accord with the laws of historical development. They have existed and will continue to exist, flourish, and develop as long as they are not contrary to national policy.

The second type of guerrilla warfare directly contradicts the law of historical development. Of this type, we may cite the examples furnished by the White Russian guerrilla units organized by Denikin and Kolchak; those organized by the Japanese; those organized by the Italians in Abyssinia; those supported by the puppet governments in Manchuria and Mongolia, and those that will be organized here by Chinese traitors. All such have oppressed the masses and have been contrary to the true interests of the people. They must be firmly opposed. They are easy to destroy because they lack a broad foundation in the people.

If we fail to differentiate between the two types of guerrilla hostilities mentioned, it is likely that we will exaggerate their effect when applied by an invader. We might arrive at the conclusion that 'the invader can organize guerrilla units from among the people'. Such a conclusion might well diminish our confidence in guerrilla warfare. As far as this matter is concerned, we have but to remember the historical experience of revolutionary struggles.

Further, we must distinguish general revolutionary wars from those of a purely 'class' type. In the former case, the whole people of a nation, without regard to class or party, carry on a guerrilla struggle that is an instrument of the national policy. Its basis is, therefore, much broader than is the basis of a struggle of class type. Of a general guerrilla war, it has been said: 'When a nation is invaded, the people become sympathetic to one another and all aid in organizing guerrilla units. In civil war, no matter to what extent guerrillas are developed, they do not produce the same results as when they are formed to resist an invasion by foreigners. The one strong feature of guerrilla warfare in a civil struggle is its quality of internal purity. One class may be easily united and perhaps fight with great effect, whereas in a national revolutionary war, guerrilla units are faced with the problem of internal unification of different class groups. This necessitates the use of propaganda. Both types of guerrilla war are, however, similar in that they both employ the same military methods.

National guerrilla warfare, though historically of the same consistency, has employed varying implements as times, peoples, and conditions differ. The guerrilla aspects of the Opium War, those of the fighting in Manchuria since the Mukden incident, and those employed in China today are all slightly different. The guerrilla warfare conducted by the Moroccans against the French and the Spanish was not exactly similar to that which we conduct today in China. These differences express the characteristics of different peoples in different periods. Although there is a general similarity in the quality of all these struggles, there are dissimilarities in form. This fact we must recognize. Clausewitz wrote, in *On War*: 'Wars in every period have independent forms and independent conditions, and, therefore, every period must have its independent theory of war.' Lenin, in *On Guerrilla Warfare* said: 'As regards the form of fighting, it is unconditionally requisite that history be investigated in order to discover the conditions of environment, the state of economic progress and the political ideas that obtained, the national characteristics, customs, and degree of civilization.' Again: 'It is necessary to be completely unsympathetic to abstract formulas and rules and to study with sympathy the conditions of the actual fighting, for these will change in accordance with the political and economic situations and the realization of the people's aspirations. These progressive changes in conditions create new methods.'

If, in today's struggle, we fail to apply the historical truths of revolutionary guerrilla war, we will fall into the error of believing with T'ou Hsi Sheng that under the impact of Japan's mechanized army, 'the guerrilla unit has lost its historical function'. Jen Ch'i Shan writes: 'In olden days guerrilla warfare was part of regular strategy but there is almost no chance that it can be applied today.' These opinions are harmful. If we do not make an estimate of the characteristics peculiar to our anti-Japanese guerrilla war, but insist on applying to it mechanical formulas derived from past history, we are making the mistake of placing our hostilities in the same category as all other national guerrilla struggles. If we hold this view, we will simply be beating our heads against a stone wall and we will be unable to profit from guerrilla hostilities.

To summarize: What is the guerrilla war of resistance against Japan? It is one aspect of the entire war, which, although alone incapable of producing the decision, attacks the enemy in every quarter, diminishes the extent of area under his control, increases our national strength, and assists our regular armies. It is one of the strategic instruments used to inflict defeat on our enemy. It is the one pure expression of anti-Japanese policy, that is to say, it is military strength organized by the active people and inseparable from them. It is a powerful special weapon with which we resist the Japanese and without which we cannot defeat them.

# CHAPTER 2

# The Relation of Guerrilla Hostilities to Regular Operations

The general features of orthodox hostilities, that is, the war of position and the war of movement, differ fundamentally from guerrilla warfare. There are other readily apparent differences such as those in organization, armament, equipment supply, tactics, command; in conception of the terms 'front' and 'rear'; in the matter of military responsibilities.

When considered from the point of view of total numbers, guerrilla units are many, as individual combat units, they may vary in size from the smallest, of several score or several hundred men, to the battalion or the regiment, of several thousand. This is not the case in regularly organized units. A primary feature of guerrilla operations is their dependence upon the people themselves to organize battalions and other units. As a result of this, organization depends largely upon local circumstances. In the case of guerrilla groups, the standard of equipment is of a low order and they must depend for their sustenance primarily upon what the locality affords.

The strategy of guerrilla warfare is manifestly unlike that employed in orthodox operations, as the basic tactic of the former is constant activity and movement. There is in guerrilla warfare no such thing as a decisive battle; there is nothing comparable to the fixed, passive defense that characterizes orthodox war. In guerrilla warfare, the transformation of a moving situation into a positional defensive situation never arises. The general features of reconnaissance, partial deployment, general deployment, and development of the attack that are usual in mobile warfare are not common in guerrilla war.

There are differences also in the matter of leadership and command. In guerrilla warfare, small units acting independently play the principal role and there must be no excessive interference with their activities. In orthodox warfare particularly in a moving situation, a certain degree of initiative is accorded subordinates, but in principle, command is centralized. This is done because all units and all supporting arms in all districts must co-ordinate to the highest degree. In the case of guerrilla warfare, this is not only undesirable but impossible. Only adjacent guerrilla units can coordinate their activities to any degree. Strategically, their activities can be roughly correlated with those of the regular forces, and tactically, they must co-operate with adjacent units of the regular army. But there are no strictures on the extent of guerrilla activity nor is it primarily characterized by the quality of co-operation of many units.

When we discuss the terms 'front' and 'rear' it must be remembered, that while guerrillas do have bases, their primary field of activity is in the enemy's rear areas. They themselves have no rear. Because an orthodox army has rear installations (except in some special cases as during the 10,000-mile Long march of the Red Army or as in the case of certain units operating in Shansi Province), it cannot operate as guerrillas can.

As to the matter of military responsibilities, those of the guerrillas are to exterminate small forces of the enemy; to harass and weaken large forces; to attack enemy lines of communications; to establish bases capable of supporting independent operations in the enemy's rear, to force the enemy to disperse his strength; and to co-ordinate all these activities with those of the regular armies on distant battle fronts.

From the foregoing summary of differences that exist between guerrilla warfare and orthodox warfare, it can be seen that it is improper to compare the two. Further distinction must be made in order to clarify this matter. While the Eighth Route Army is a regular army, its North China campaign is essentially guerrilla in nature, for it operates in enemy's rear. On occasion, however, Eighth Route Army commanders have concentrated powerful forces to strike an enemy in motion and the characteristics of orthodox mobile warfare were evident in the battle at P'ing Hsing Kuan and in other engagements.

On the other hand, after the fall of Feng Ling Tu, the operations of Central Shansi, and Suiyuan, troops were more guerrilla than orthodox in nature. In this connection the precise character of Generalissimo Chiang's instructions to the effect that independent brigades would carry out guerrilla operations should be recalled. In spite of such temporary activities these orthodox units retained their identity and after the fall of Feng Line Tu, they were not only able to fight along orthodox lines but often found it necessary to do so. This is an example of the fact that orthodox armies may, due to changes in the situation, temporarily function as guerrillas.

Likewise, guerrilla units formed from the people may gradually develop into regular units and, when operating as such, employ the tactics of orthodox mobile war. While these units function as guerrillas, they may be compared to innumerable gnats, which, by biting a giant both in front and in rear, ultimately exhaust him. They make themselves as unendurable as a group of cruel and hateful devils, and as they grow and attain gigantic proportions, they will find that their victim is not only exhausted but practically perishing. It is for this very reason that our guerrilla activities are a source of constant mental worry to Imperial Japan.

While it is improper to confuse orthodox with guerrilla operations, it is equally improper to consider that there is a chasm between the two. While differences do exist, similarities appear under certain conditions and this fact must be appreciated if we wish to establish clearly the relationship between the two. If we consider both types of warfare as a single subject, or if we confuse guerrilla warfare with the mobile operations of orthodox war, we fall into this error: We exaggerate the function of guerrillas and minimize that of the regular armies. If we agree with Chang Tso Hua, who says - 'Guerrilla warfare is the primary war strategy of a people seeking to emancipate itself,' or with Kao Kang, who believes that 'Guerrilla strategy is the only strategy possible for oppressed people', we are exaggerating the importance of guerrilla hostilities. What these zealous friends I have just quoted do not realize is this: If we do not fit guerrilla operations into their proper niche, we cannot promote them realistically. Then, not only would those who oppose take advantage of our varying opinions to turn them to the own uses to undermine us, but guerrillas would be led assume responsibilities they could not successfully discharge and that should properly be carried out by orthodox force. In the meantime, the important guerrilla function of co-ordinating activities with the regular forces would be neglected.

Furthermore, if the theory that guerrilla warfare is our only strategy were actually applied, the regular forces would be weakened, we would be divided in purpose, and guerrilla hostilities would decline. If we say, ' Let us transform the regular forces into guerrillas', and do not place our first reliance on a victory to be gained by the regular armies over the enemy, we may certainly expect to see as a result the failure of the anti-Japanese war of resistance. The concept that guerrilla warfare is an end in itself and that guerrilla activities can be divorced from those of the regular forces is incorrect. If we assume that guerrilla warfare does not progress from beginning to end beyond its elementary forms, we have failed to recognize the fact that guerrilla hostilities can, under specific conditions, develop and assume orthodox characteristics. An opinion that admits the existence of guerrilla war, but isolates it, is one that does not properly estimate the potentialities of such war.

Equally dangerous is the concept that condemns guerrilla war on the ground that war has no other aspects than the purely orthodox. This opinion is often expressed by those who have seen the corrupt phenomena of some guerrilla regimes, observed their lack of discipline, and have seen them used as a screen behind which certain persons have indulged in bribery and other corrupt practices. These people will not admit the fundamental necessity for guerrilla bands that spring from the armed people. They say, 'Only the regular forces are capable of conducting guerrilla operations.' This theory is a mistaken one and would lead to the abolition of the people's guerrilla war.

A proper conception of the relationship that exists between guerrilla effort and that of the regular forces is essential. We believe it can be stated this way: 'Guerrilla operations during the anti-Japanese war may for certain time and temporarily become its paramount feature, particularly insofar as the enemy's rear is concerned. However, if we view the war as a whole, there can be no doubt that our regular forces are of primary importance, because it is they who are alone capable of producing the decision. Guerrilla warfare assists them in producing this favorable decision. Orthodox forces may under certain conditions operate as guerrillas, and the latter may, under certain conditions, develop to the status of the former. However, both guerrilla forces and regular forces have their own respective development and their proper combinations.'

To clarify the relationship between the mobile aspect of orthodox war and guerrilla war, we may say that general agreement exists that the principal element of our strategy must be mobility. With the war of movement, we may at times combine the war of position. Both of these are assisted by general guerrilla hostilities. It is true that on the battlefield mobile war often becomes positional; it is true that this situation may be reversed; it is equally true that each form may combine with the other. The possibility of such combination will become more evident after the prevailing standards of equipment have been raised. For example, in a general strategic counter-attack to recapture key cities and lines of communication, it would be normal to use both mobile and positional methods. However, the point must again be made that our fundamental strategic form must be the war of movement. If we deny this, we cannot arrive at the victorious solution of the war. In sum, while we must promote guerrilla warfare as a necessary strategic auxiliary to orthodox operations, we must neither assign it the primary position in our war strategy nor substitute it for mobile and positional warfare as conducted by orthodox forces.

# CHAPTER 3

# Guerrilla Warfare in History

Guerrilla warfare is neither a product of China nor peculiar to the present day. From the earliest historical days, it has been a feature of wars fought by every class of men against invaders and oppressors. Under suitable conditions, it has great possibilities. The many guerrilla wars in history have their points of difference, their peculiar characteristics, their varying processes and conclusions, and we must respect and profit by the experience of those whose blood was shed in them. What a pity it is that the priceless experience gained during the several hundred wars waged by the peasants of China cannot be marshaled today to guide us. Our only experience in guerrilla hostilities has been that gained from the several conflicts that have been carried on against us by foreign imperialists. But that experience should help the fighting Chinese recognize the necessity for guerrilla warfare and should confirm them in confidence of ultimate victory.

In September 1812, Napoleon, in the course of swallowing all of Europe, invaded Russia at the head of a great army totaling several hundred thousand infantry, cavalry, and artillery. At that time, Russia was weak and her ill-prepared army was not concentrated. The most important phase of her strategy was the use made of Cossack cavalry and detachments of peasants to carry on guerrilla operations. After giving up Moscow, the Russians formed nine guerrilla divisions of about five hundred men each. These, and vast groups of organized peasants, carried on partisan warfare and continually harassed the French Army. When the French Army was withdrawing, cold and starving, Russian guerrillas blocked the way and, in combination with regular troops, carried out counterattacks on the French rear, pursuing and defeating them. The army of the heroic Napoleon was almost entirely annihilated, and the guerrillas captured many officers, men, cannon, and rifles. Though the victory was the result of various factors and depended largely on the activities of the regular army the function of the partisan groups was extremely important. The corrupt and poorly organized country that was Russia defeated and destroyed an army led by the most famous soldier of Europe and won the war in spite of the fact that her ability to organize guerrilla regimes was not fully developed. At times, guerrilla groups were hindered in their operations and the supply of equipment and arms was insufficient. If we use the Russian saying, it was a case of a battle between "the fist and the axe."

From 1918 to 1920, the Russian Soviets, because of the opposition and intervention of foreign imperialists and the internal disturbances of White Russian groups, were forced to organize themselves in occupied territories and fight a real war. In Siberia and Alashan, in the rear of the army of the traitor Denikin and in the rear of the Poles, there were many Red Russian guerrillas. These not only disrupted and destroyed the communications in the enemy's rear but also frequently prevented his advance. On one occasion, the guerrillas completely destroyed a retreating White Army that had previously been defeated by regular Red forces. Kolchak, Denikin, the Japanese, and the Poles, owing to the necessity of staving off the attacks of guerrillas, were forced to withdraw regular troops from the front. 'Thus not only was the enemy's manpower impoverished but he found himself unable to cope with the ever-moving guerrilla'.

The development of guerrillas at that time had only reached the stage where there were detached groups of several thousands in strength, old, middle-aged, and young. The old men organized themselves into propaganda groups known as 'silver-haired units'; there was a suitable guerrilla activity for the middle-aged; the young men formed combat units, and there were even groups for the children. Among the leaders were determined Communists who carried on general political work among the people. These, although they opposed the doctrine of extreme guerrilla warfare, were quick to oppose those who condemned it. Experience tells us that 'Orthodox armies are the fundamental and principal power, guerrilla units are secondary to them and assist in the accomplishment of the mission assigned the regular forces *[Gusev, Lessons of Civil War.]*. Many of the guerrilla regimes in Russia gradually developed until in battle they were able to discharge functions of organized regulars. The army of the famous General Galen was entirely derived from guerrillas.

During seven months in 1935 and 1936, the Abyssinians lost their war against Italy. The cause of defeat — aside from the most important political reasons that there were dissentient political groups, no strong government party, and unstable policy—was the failure to adopt a positive policy of mobile warfare. There was never a combination of the war of movement with large-scale guerrilla operations. Ultimately, the Abyssinians adopted a purely passive defense, with the result that they were unable to defeat the Italians. In addition to this, the fact that Abyssinia is a relatively small and sparsely populated country was contributory. Even in spite of the fact that the Abyssinian Army and its equipment were not modern, she was able to withstand a mechanized Italian force of 400,000 for seven months. During that period, there were several occasions when a war of movement was combined with large-scale guerrilla operations to strike the Italians heavy blows. Moreover, several cities were retaken and casualties totaling 140,000 were inflicted. Had this policy been steadfastly continued, it would have been difficult to have named the ultimate winner. At the present time, guerrilla activities continue in Abyssinia, and if the internal political questions can be solved, an extension of such activities is probable.

In 1841 and 1842, when brave people from San Yuan Li fought the English; again from 1850 to 1864, during the Taiping War, and for a third time in 1899 in the Boxer Uprising, guerrilla tactics were employed to a remarkable degree. Particularly was this so during the Taiping War, when guerrilla operations were most extensive and the Ch'ing troops were often completely exhausted and forced to flee for their lives.

In these wars, there were no guiding principles of guerrilla action. Perhaps these guerrilla hostilities were not carried out in conjunction with regular operations, or perhaps there was a lack of co-ordination. But the fact that victory was not gained was not because of any lack in guerrilla activity but rather because of the interference of politics in military affairs. Experience shows that if precedence is not given to the question of conquering the enemy in both political and military affairs, and if regular hostilities are not conducted with tenacity, guerrilla operations alone cannot produce final victory.

From 1927 to 1936, the Chinese Red Army fought almost continually and employed guerrilla tactics contently. At the very beginning, a positive policy was adopted. Many bases were established, and from guerrilla bands, the Reds were able to develop into regular armies. As these armies fought, new guerrilla regimes were developed over a wide area. These regimes co-ordinated their efforts with those of the regular forces This policy accounted for the many victories gained by the guerrilla troops relatively few in number, who were armed with weapons inferior to those of their opponents. The leaders of that period properly combined guerrilla operations with a war of movement both strategically and tactically. They depended primarily upon alertness. They stressed the correct basis for both political affairs and military operations. They developed their guerrilla bands into trained units. They then determined upon a ten year period of resistance during which time they overcame innumerable difficulties and have only lately reached their goal of direct participation in the anti-Japanese war. There is no doubt that the internal unification of China is now a permanent and definite fact, and that the experience gained during our internal struggles has proved to be both necessary and advantageous to us in the struggle against Japanese imperialism. There are many valuable lessons we can learn from the experience of those years. Principle among them is the fact that guerrilla success largely depend upon powerful political leaders who work unceasingly to bring about internal unification. Such leaders must work with the people; they must have a correct conception of the policy to be adopted as regards both the people and the enemy.

After 18 September 1931, strong anti-Japanese guerrilla campaigns were opened in each of the three north-east provinces. Guerrilla activity persists there in spite of the cruelties and deceits practiced by the Japanese at the expense of the people, and in spite of the fact that her armies have occupied the land and oppressed the people for the last seven years. The struggle can be divided into two periods. During the first, which extended from 18 September 1931 to January 1933, anti-Japanese guerrilla activity exploded constantly in all three provinces. Ma Chan Shan and Su Ping Wei established an anti-Japanese regime in Heilungkiang. In Chi Lin. the National Salvation Army and the Self-Defense Army were led by Wang Te Lin and Li Tu respectively. In Feng T'ien, Chu Lu and others commanded guerrilla units. The influence of these forces was great. They harassed the Japanese unceasingly, but because there was an indefinite political goal, improper leadership, failure to co ordinate military command and operations and to work with the people, and, finally, failure to delegate proper political functions to the army, the whole organization was feeble, and its strength was not unified. As a direct result of these conditions, the campaigns failed and the troops were finally defeated by our enemy.

During the second period, which has extended from January 1933 to the present time, the situation has greatly improved, This has come about because great numbers of people who have been oppressed by the enemy have decided to resist him, because of the participation of the Chinese Communists in the anti-Japanese warm and because of the fine work of the volunteer units. The guerrillas have finally educated the people to the meaning of guerrilla warfare, and in the north-east, it has again become an important and powerful influence. Already seven or eight guerrilla regiments and a number of independent platoons have been formed, and their activities make it necessary for the Japanese to send troops after them month after month. These units hamper the Japanese and undermine their control in the north-east, while, at the same time they inspire a Nationalist revolution in Korea. Such activities are not merely of transient and local importance but directly contribute to our ultimate victory.

However, there are still some weak points. For instance: National defense policy has not been sufficiently developed; participation of the people is not general; internal political organization is still in its primary stages, and the force used to attack the Japanese and the puppet governments is not yet sufficient. But if present policy is continued tenaciously, all these weaknesses will be overcome. Experience proves that guerrilla war will develop to even greater proportions and that, in spite of the cruelty o the Japanese and the many methods they have device to cheat the people, they cannot extinguish guerrilla activities extinguish guerrilla activities in the three north-eastern provinces.

The guerrilla experiences of China and of other countries that have been outlined; prove that in a war of revolutionary nature such hostilities are possible, natural and necessary. They prove that if the present anti-Japanese war for the emancipation of the masses of the Chinese people is to gain ultimate victory, such hostilities must expand tremendously.

Historical experience is written in iron and blood. We must point out that the guerrilla campaigns being waged in China today are a page in history that has no precedent. Their influence will not be confined solely to China in her present anti-Japanese war but will be world-wide.

# CHAPTER 4

# Can Victory Be Attained By Guerrilla Operations?

Guerrilla hostilities are but one phase of the war of resistance against Japan and the answer to the question of whether or not they can produce ultimate victory can be given only after investigation and comparison of all elements of our own strength with those of the enemy. The particulars of such a comparison are several. First, the strong Japanese bandit nation is an absolute monarchy. During the course of her invasion of China, she had made comparative progress in the techniques of industrial production and in the development of excellence and skill in her army, navy, and air force. But in spite of this industrial progress, she remains an absolute monarchy of inferior physical endowments. Her manpower, her raw materials, and her financial resources are all inadequate and insufficient to maintain her in protracted warfare or to meet the situation presented by a war prosecuted over a vast area. Added to this is the anti-war feeling now manifested by the Japanese people, a feeling that is shared by the junior officers and, more extensively, by the soldiers of the invading army. Furthermore, China is not Japan's only enemy. Japan is unable to employ her entire strength in the attack on China; she cannot, at most, spare more than a million men for this purpose, as she must hold any in excess of that number for use against other possible opponents. Because of these important primary considerations, the invading Japanese bandits can hope neither to be victorious in a protracted struggle nor to conquer a vast area. Their strategy must be one of lightning war and speedy decision. If we can hold out for three or more years, it will be most difficult for Japan to bear up under the strain.

In the war, the Japanese brigands must depend upon lines of communication linking the principal cities as routes for the transport of war materials. The most important considerations for her are that her rear be stable and peaceful and that her lines of communication be intact. It is not to her an advantage to wage war over a vast area with disrupted lines of communication. She cannot disperse her strength and fight in a number of places, and her greatest fears are these eruptions in her rear and disruption of her lines of communication. If she can maintain communications, she will be able at will to concentrate powerful forces speedily at strategic points to engage our organized units in decisive battle. Another important Japanese objective is to profit from the industries, finances, and manpower in captured areas and with them to augment her own insufficient strength. Certainly, it is not to her advantage to forgo these benefits, not to be forced to dissipate her energies in a type of warfare in which the gains will not compensate for the losses. It is for these reasons that guerrilla warfare conducted in each bit of conquered territory over a wide area will be a heavy blow struck at the Japanese bandits. Experience in the five northern provinces as well as in Kiangsu, Chekiang and Anhwei has absolutely established the truth of this assertion.

China is a country half colonial and half feudal; it is a country that is politically, militarily, and economically backward. This is an inescapable conclusion. It is a vast country with great resources and tremendous population, a country in which the terrain is complicated and the facilities for communication are poor. All theses factors favor a protracted war; they all favor the application of mobile warfare and guerilla operations. The establishment of innumerable anti-Japanese bases behind the enemy's lines will force him to fight unceasingly in many places at once, both to his front and his rear. He thus endlessly expends his resources.

We must unite the strength of the army with that of the people, we must strike the weak spots in the enemy's flanks, in his front, in his rear. We must make war everywhere and cause dispersal of his forces and dissipation of his strength. Thus the time will come when a gradual change will become evident in the relative position of ourselves and our enemy, and when that day comes, it will be the beginning of our ultimate victory over the Japanese.

Although China's population is great, it is unorganized. This is a weakness which must be then into account.

The Japanese bandits have merely to conquer territory; but continue with a murderous policy of the extinction of the Chinese race. We must unite the nation without regard to parties and follow our policy of resistance to the end. China today is not the China of old. It is not like Abyssinia. China today is at the point of her greatest historical progress. The standards of literacy among the masses have been raised; the *rapprochement* of Communists and Nationalists has laid the foundation for an anti-Japanese war front that is constantly being strengthened and expanded; government, army and people are all working with great energy; the raw material resources and the economic strength of the nation are waiting to be used; the unorganized people are becoming an organized nation.

These energies must be directed toward the goal of protracted war so that should the Japanese occupy much of our territory or even most of it, we shall still gain final victory. Not only must those behind our lines organize for resistance but also those who live in Japanese-occupied territory in every part of the country. The traitors who accept the Japanese as fathers are few in number, and those who have taken oath that they would prefer death to abject slavery are many. If we resist with this spirit, what enemy can we not conquer and who can say that ultimate victory will not be ours?

The Japanese are waging a barbaric war along uncivilized lines. For that reason, Japanese of all classes oppose the policies of their government, as do vast international groups. On the other hand, because China's cause is righteous, our countrymen of all classes and parties are united to oppose the invader; we have sympathy in many foreign countries including even Japan itself. This is perhaps the most important reason why Japan will lose and China will win.

The progress of the war for the emancipation of the Chinese people will be in accord with these facts. The guerrilla war of resistance will be in accord with these facts, and that guerrilla operations correlated with those of our regular forces will produce victory is the conviction of the many patriots who devote their entire strength to guerrilla hostilities.

# CHAPTER 5

# Organization for Guerilla Warfare

Four points must be considered. These are:

How are guerrilla bands formed?
How are guerrilla bands organized?
What are the methods of arming guerrilla bands?
What elements constitute a guerrilla band?

These are all questions pertaining to the organization armed guerrilla units; they are questions which those who had no experience in guerilla hostilities do not understand and on which they can arrive at no sound decisions; indeed, they would not know in what manner to begin.

## How Guerrilla Units Are Originally Formed

The unit may originate in any one of the following ways:

a) From the masses of the people.
b) From regular army units temporarily detailed for the purpose.
c) From regular army units permanently detailed.
d) From the combination of a regular army unit and a unit recruited from the people.
e) From the local militia.
f) From deserters from the ranks of the enemy.
g) From former bandits and bandit groups.

In the present hostilities, no doubt, all these sources will be employed.

In the first case above, the guerrilla unit is formed from the people. This is the fundamental type. Upon the arrival of the enemy army to oppress and slaughter the people, their leaders call upon them to resist. They assemble the most valorous elements, arm them with old rifles or whatever firearms they can, and thus a guerrilla unit begins. Orders have already been issued throughout the nation, that call upon the people to form guerrilla units both for local defense and for other combat. If the local governments approve and aid such movements, they cannot fail to prosper. In some places, where the local government is not determined or where its officers have all fled, the leaders among the masses (relying on the sympathy of the people and their sincere desire to resist Japan and succor the country) call upon the people to resist, and they respond. Thus, many guerrilla units are organized. In circumstances of this kind, the duties of leadership usually fall upon the shoulders of young students, teachers, professors, other educators, local soldiery, professional men, artisans, and those without a fixed profession, who are willing to exert themselves to the last drop of their blood. Recently, in Shansi, Hopeh, Chahar, Suiyuan, Shantung, Chekiang, Anhwei, Kiangsu, and other provinces, extensive guerrilla hostilities have broken out. All these are organized and led by patriots. The amount of such activity is the best proof of the foregoing statement. The more such bands there are, the better will the situation be. Each district, each county, should be able to organize a great number of guerrilla squads, which, when assembled, form a guerrilla company.

There are those who say: 'I am a farmer', or, 'I am a student'; 'I can discuss literature but not military arts.' This is incorrect. There is no profound difference between the farmer and the soldier. You must have courage. You simply leave your farms and become soldiers. That you are farmers is of no difference, and if you have education, that is so much the better. When you take your arms in hand, you become soldiers; when you are organized, you become military units.

Guerrilla hostilities are the university of war, and after you have fought several times valiantly and aggressively, you may become a leader of troops and there will be many well-known regular soldiers who will not be your peers. Without question, the fountainhead of guerrilla warfare is in the masses of the people, who organize guerrilla units directly from themselves.

The second type of guerrilla unit is that which is organized from small units of the regular forces temporarily detached for the purpose. For example, since hostilities commenced, many groups have been temporarily detached from armies, divisions, and brigades and have been assigned guerrilla duties. A regiment of the regular army may, if circumstances warrant, be dispersed into groups for the purpose of carrying on guerrilla operations. As an example of this, there is the Eighth Route Army, in North China. Excluding the periods when it carries on mobile operations as an army, it is divided into its elements and these carry on guerrilla hostilities. This type of guerrilla unit is essential for two reasons. First, in mobile-warfare situations, the co-ordination of guerrilla activities with regular operations is necessary. Second, until guerrilla hostilities can be developed on a grand scale, there is no one to carry out guerrilla missions but regulars. Historical experience shows us that regular army units are not able to undergo the hardships of guerrilla campaigning over long periods. The leaders of regular units engaged in guerrilla operations must be extremely adaptable. They must study the methods of guerrilla war. They must understand that initiative, discipline, and the employment of stratagems are all of the utmost importance. As the guerrilla status of regular units is but temporary, their leaders must lend all possible support to the organization of guerrilla units from among the people. These units must be so disciplined that they hold together after the departure of the regulars.

The third type of unit consists of a detachment of regulars who are permanently assigned guerrilla duties. This type of small detachment does not have to be prepared to rejoin the regular forces. Its post is somewhere in the rear of the enemy, and there it becomes the backbone of guerrilla organization. As an example of this type of organization we may take the Wu Tat Shan district in the heart of the Hopeh-Chahar-Shansi area. Along the borders of these provinces, units from the Eighth Route Army have established a framework or guerrilla operations. Around these small cores, many detachments have been organized and the area of guerrilla activity greatly expanded. In areas in which there is a possibility of cutting the enemy's lines of supply, this system should be used. Severing enemy, supply routes destroys his lifeline; this is one feature that cannot be neglected. If, at the time the regular forces withdraw from a certain area, some units left behind, these should conduct guerrilla operations in the enemy's rear. As an example of this, we have the guerrilla bands now continuing their independent operations in the Shanghai-Woosung area in spite of the withdrawal of regular forces.

The fourth type of organization is the result of a merger between small regular detachments and local guerrilla units. The regular forces may dispatch a squad, a platoon, or a company, which is placed at the disposal of the local guerrilla commander. If a small group experienced in military and political affairs is sent, it becomes the core of the local guerrilla unit. These several methods are all excellent, and if properly applied, the intensity of guerilla warfare can be extended. In the Wu Tat Shan area, each of these methods has been used.

The fifth type mentioned above is from the local militia, from police and home guards. In every North China province, there are now many of these groups, and they should be formed in every locality. The government has issued mandate to the effect that the people are not to depart from war areas. The officer in command of the county, the commander of the peace-preservation unit, the chief of police are all required to obey this mandate. They cannot retreat with their forces but must remain at their stations and resist.

The sixth type of unit is that organized from troops that come over from the enemy—the Chinese 'traitor' troops employed by the Japanese. It is always possible to produce disaffection in their ranks, and we must increase our propaganda efforts and foment mutinies among such troops. Immediately after mutinying, they must be received into our ranks and organized. The concord of the leaders and the assent of the men must be gained, and the units rebuilt politically and reorganized militarily. Once this has been accomplished, they become successful guerrilla units. In regard to this type of unit, it may be said that political work among them is of utmost importance.

The seventh type of guerrilla organization is that formed from bands of bandits and brigands. This, although difficult, must be carried out with utmost vigor lest the enemy use such bands to his own advantages. Many bandit groups pose as anti-Japanese guerrillas, and it is only necessary to correct their political beliefs to convert them.

In spite of inescapable differences in the fundamental types of guerrilla bands, it is possible to unite them to form a vast sea of guerrillas. The ancients said, 'Tai Shan is a great mountain because it does not scorn the merest handful of dirt; the rivers and seas are deep because they absorb the waters of small streams.' Attention paid to the enlistment and organization of guerrillas of every type and from every source will increase the potentialities of guerrilla action in the anti-Japanese war. This is something that patriots will not neglect.

# THE METHOD OF ORGANIZING GUERRILLA REGIMES

Many of those who decide to participate in guerrilla activities do not know the methods of organization. For such people, as well as for students who have no knowledge of military affairs, the matter of organization is a problem that requires solution. Even among those who have military knowledge, there are some who know nothing of guerrilla regimes use they are lacking in that particular type of experience. The subject of the organization of such regimes is not confined to the organization of specific units but includes all guerrilla activities within the area where the regime functions.

As an example of such organization, we may take a geographical area in the enemy's rear. This area may comprise many counties. It must be sub-divided and individual companies or battalions formed to accord with the sub-divisions. To this 'military area', a military commander and political commissioners are appointed. Under these, the necessary officers both military and political, are appointed. In the military headquarters, there will be the staff, the aides, the supply officers, and the medical personnel. These are controlled by the chief of staff, who acts in accordance with orders from the commander. In the political headquarters, there are bureaus of propaganda organization, people's mass movements, and miscellaneous affairs. Control of these is vested in the political chairman.

The military areas are sub-divided into smaller districts in accordance with local geography, the enemy situation locally, and the state of guerrilla development. Each of these smaller divisions within the area is a district, each of which may consist of from two to six counties. To each district, a military commander and several political commissioners are appointed. Under their direction, military and political headquarters are organized. Tasks are assigned in accordance with the number of guerrilla troops available. Although the names of the officers in the 'district' correspond to those in the larger 'area', the number of the functionaries assigned in the former case should be reduced to the least possible. In order to unify control, to handle guerrilla troops that come from different sources, and to harmonize military operations and local political affairs, a committee of from seven to nine members should be organized in each area and district. This committee, the members of which are selected by the troops and the local political officers, should function as a forum for the discussion of both military and political matters.

All the people in an area should arm themselves and be organized into two groups. One of these groups is a combat group, the other a self-defense unit with but limited military quality. Regular combatant guerrillas are organized into one of three general types of units. The first of these is the small unit, the platoon or company. In each county, three to six units may be organized. The second type is the battalion of from two to four companies. One such unit should be organized in each county. While the unit fundamentally belongs to the county in it was organized, it may operate in other counties. While in areas other than its own, it must operate in conjunction with local units in order to take advantage of their manpower, their knowledge of local terrain and local customs, and their information of the enemy.

The third type is the guerrilla regiment, which consists of from two to four of the above-mentioned battalion units. If sufficient manpower is available, a guerrilla a brigade of from two to four regiments may be formed.

Each of the units has its own peculiarities of organization. A squad, the smallest unit, has a strength of from nine to eleven men, including the leader and the assistant leader. Its arms may be from two to five Western-style rifles, with the remaining men armed with rifles of local manufacture, fowling-pieces, etc., spears, or big swords. Two to four such squads form a platoon. This too has a leader and an assistant leader, and when acting independently, it is assigned a political officer to carry on political propaganda work. The platoon may have about ten rifles, with the remainder of its four of such units from a company, which, like the platoon, has a leader, an assistant leader, and a political officer. All these units are under the direct supervision of the military commanders of the areas in which they operate.

The battalion unit must be more thoroughly organized and better equipped than the smaller units. Its discipline and its personnel should be superior. If a battalion is formed from company units, it should not deprive subordinate units entirely of their manpower and their arms. If in a small area, there is a peace-preservation corps, a branch of the militia, or police, regular guerrilla units should not be dispersed over it.

The guerrilla unit next in size to the battalion is the regiment. This must be under more severe discipline than the battalion. In an independent guerrilla regiment, there may be ten men per squad, three squad per platoon, three platoons per company, three companies per battalion, and three battalions to the regiment. Two of such regiments form a brigade. Each of these units has a commander, a vice-commander, and a political officer.

In North China, guerrilla cavalry units should be established. These may be regiments of from two to four companies, or battalions.

All these units from the lowest to the highest are combatant guerrilla units and receive their supplies from the central government. Details of their organization are shown in the tables.

All the people of both sexes from the ages of sixteen to forty-five must be organized into anti-Japanese self-defense units, the basis of which is voluntary service. As a first step, they must procure arms, then they must be given both military and political training. Their responsibilities are: local sentry duties, securing information of the enemy, arresting traitors, and preventing the dissemination of enemy propaganda. When the enemy launches a guerrilla-suppression drive, these units, armed with what weapons there are, are assigned to certain areas to deceive, hinder, and harass him. Thus, the defense units assist the combatant guerrillas. They have other functions. They furnish stretcher-bearers to transport the wounded, carriers to take food to the troops, and comfort missions to provide the troops with tea and rice. If a locality can organize such a self-defense unit as we have described, the traitors cannot hide nor can bandits and robbers disturb the peace of the people. Thus the people will continue to assist the guerrilla and supply manpower to our regular armies. 'The organization of self-defense units is a transitional step in the development of universal conscription. Such units are reservoirs of manpower for the orthodox forces.'

There have been such organizations for some time in Shansi, Shensi, Honan, and Suiyuan. The youth organizations in different provinces were formed for the purpose of educating the young. They have been of some help. However, they were not voluntary, and confidence of the people was thus not gained. These organizations were not widespread, and their effect was almost negligible. This system was, therefore, supplanted by the new-type organizations,. Which are organized on the principles of voluntary co-operation and non-separation of the members from their native localities. When the members of these organizations are in their native towns, they support themselves. Only in case of military necessity are they ordered to remote places, and when this is done, the government must support them. Each member of these groups must have a weapon even if the weapon is only a knife, a pistol, a lance, or a spear.

In all places where the enemy operates, these self-defense units should organize within themselves a small guerrilla group of perhaps from three to ten men armed with pistols or revolvers. This group is not required to leave its native locality.

The organization of these self-defense units is mentioned in this book because such units are useful for the purposes of inculcating the people with military and political knowledge, keeping order in the rear, and replenishing the ranks of the regulars. These groups should be organized not only in the active war zones but in every province in China. 'The people must be inspired to co-operate voluntarily. We must not force them, for if we do, it will be ineffectual.' This is extremely important.

In order to control anti-Japanese military organization as a whole, it is necessary to establish a system of military areas and districts along the lines we have indicated.

# EQUIPMENT OF GUERRILLAS

In regard to the problem of guerrilla equipment, it must be understood that guerrillas are lightly-armed attack groups, which require simple equipment. The standard of equipment is based upon the nature of duties assigned; the equipment of low-class guerrilla units is not as good as that of higher-class units. For example, those who are assigned the task of destroying rail communications are better equipped than those who do not have that task. The equipment of guerrillas cannot be based on what the guerrillas want, to even what they need, but must be based on what is available for their use. Equipment cannot be furnished immediately but must be acquired gradually. These are points to be kept in mind.

The question of equipment includes the collection, supply, distribution, and replacement of weapons, ammunition, blankets, communication materials, transport, and facilities for propaganda work. The supply of weapons and ammunition is most difficult, particularly at the time the unit is established, but this problem can always be solved eventually. Guerrilla bands that originate in the people are furnished with revolvers, pistols, rifles, spears, big swords, and land mines and mortars of local manufacture. Other elementary weapons are added and as many new-type rifles as are available are distributed. After a period of resistance, it is possible to increase the supply of equipment by capturing it from the enemy. In this respect, the transport companies are the easiest to equip, for in any successful attack, we will capture the enemy's transport.

An armory should be established in each guerrilla district for the manufacture and repair of rifles and for the production of cartridge, hand grenades and bayonets. Guerrillas must not depend too much on an armory. The enemy is the principal source of their supply.

For destruction of railway tracks, bridges, and stations in enemy-controlled territory, it is necessary to gather together demolition materials. Troops must be trained in the preparation and use of demolitions, and a demolition unit must be organized in each regiment.

As for minimum clothing requirements, these are that each man shall have at least two summer-weight uniforms, one suit of winter clothing, two hats, a pair of wrap puttees, and blanket. Each man must have a pack or a bag for food. In the north, each man must have an overcoat. In acquiring this clothing, we cannot depend on captures made by the enemy, for it is forbidden for captors to take clothing from their prisoners. In order to maintain high morale in guerrilla forces, all the clothing and equipment mentioned should be furnished by the representatives of the government in each guerrilla district. These men may confiscate clothing from traitors or ask contributions from those best able to afford them. In subordinate groups, uniforms are unnecessary.

Telephone and radio equipment is not necessary in lower groups, but all units from regiment up are equipped with both. This material can be obtained by contributions from the regular forces and by capture from the enemy.

In the guerrilla army in general, and at bases in particular, there must be a high standard of medical equipment. Besides the services of the doctors, medicines must be procured. Although guerrillas can depend on the enemy for some portion of their medical supplies, they must, in general, depend upon contributions. If Western medicines are not available, local medicines must be made to suffice.

The problem of transport is more vital in North-China than in the south, for in the south all that are necessary are mules and horses. Small guerrilla units need no animals, but regiments and brigades will find them necessary. Commanders and staffs of units from companies up should be furnished a riding animal each. At times, two officers will have to share a horse. Officers whose duties are of minor nature do not have to be mounted.

Propaganda materials are very important. Every large guerrilla unit should have a printing press and a mimeograph stone. They must also have paper on which to print propaganda leaflets and notices. They must be supplied with large brushes. In guerrilla areas, there should be a printing press or a lead-type press.

For the purpose of printing training instructions, this material is of the greatest importance.

In addition to the equipment listed above, it is necessary to have field-glasses, compasses, and military maps. An accomplished guerrilla group will acquire these things.

Because of the proved importance of guerrilla hostilities in the anti-Japanese war, the headquarters of the Nationalist Government and the commanding officers of the various war zones should do their best to supply the guerrillas with what they actually need and are unable to get for themselves. However, it must be repeated that guerrilla equipment will in the main depend on the efforts of the guerrillas themselves. If they depend on higher officers too much, the psychological effect will be to weaken the guerrilla spirit of resistance.

# ELEMENTS OF THE GUERRILLA ARMY

The term 'element' as used in the title to this section refers to the personnel, both officers and men, of the guerrilla army. Since each guerrilla group fights in a protracted war, its officers must be brave and positive men whose entire loyalty is dedicated to the cause of emancipation of the people. An officer should have the following qualities: great powers of endurance so that in spite of any hardship he sets an example to his men and be a model for them; he must be able to mix easily with the people; his spirit and that of the men must be one in strengthening the policy of resistance to the Japanese. If he wishes to gain victories, he must study tactics. A guerrilla group with officers of this caliber would be unbeatable. I do not mean that every guerrilla group can have, at its inception, officers of such qualities. The officers must be men naturally endowed with good qualities which can be developed during the course of campaigning. The most important natural quality is that of complete loyalty to the idea of people's emancipation. If this is present, the others will develop; if it is not present, nothing can be done. When officers are first selected from a group, it is this quality that should receive particular attention.

The officers in a group should be inhabitants of the locality in which the group is organized, as this will facilitate relations between them and the local civilians. In addition, officers so chosen would be familiar with conditions. If in any locality there are not enough men of sufficiently high qualifications to become officers, an effort must be made to train and educate the people so these qualities may be developed and the potential officer material increased. There can be no disagreements between officers native to one place and those from other localities.

A guerrilla group ought to operate on the principle that only volunteers are acceptable for service. It is a mistake to impress people into service. As long as a person is willing to fight, his social condition or position is no consideration, but only men who are courageous and determined can bear the hardships of guerrilla campaigning in a protracted war.

A soldier who habitually breaks regulations must be dismissed from the army. Vagabonds and vicious people must not be accepted for service. The opium habit must be forbidden, and a soldier who cannot break himself of the habit should be dismissed. Victory in guerrilla war is conditioned upon keeping the membership pure and clean.

It is a fact that during the war the enemy may take advantage of certain people who are lacking in conscience and patriotism and induce them to join the guerrillas for the purpose of betraying them. Officers must, therefore, continually educate the soldiers and inculcate patriotism in them. This will prevent the success of traitors. The traitors who are in the ranks must be discovered and expelled, and punishment and expulsion meted out to those who have been influenced by them. In all such cases, the officers should summon the soldiers and relate the facts to them, thus arousing their hatred and detestation for traitors. This procedure will serve as well as a warning to the other soldiers. If an officer is discovered to be a traitor, some prudence must be used in the punishment adjudged. However, the work of eliminating traitors in the army begins with their elimination from among the people.

Chinese soldiers who have served under puppet governments and bandits who have been converted should be welcomed as individuals or as groups. They should be well-treated and repatriated. But care should be used during their reorientation to distinguish those whose idea is to fight the Japanese from those who may be present for other reasons.

# CHAPTER 6

## The Political Problems of Guerrilla Warfare

I mentioned the fact that guerrilla troops should have a precise conception of the political goal of the struggle and the political organization to be used in attaining that goal. This means that both organization and discipline of guerrilla troops must be at a high level so that they can carry out the political activities that are the life of both the guerilla armies and of revolutionary warfare.

First of all, political activities depend upon the indoctrination of both military and political leaders with the idea of anti-Japanism. Through them, the idea is transmitted to the troops. One must not feel that he is anti-Japanese merely because he is a member of a guerrilla unit. The anti-Japanese idea must be an ever-present conviction, and if it is forgotten, we may succumb to the temptations of the enemy or be overcome with discouragement. In a war of long duration, those whose conviction that the people must be emancipated is not deep rooted are likely to become shaken in their faith or actually revolt. Without the general education that enables everyone to understand our goal of driving out Japanese imperialism and establishing a free and happy China, the soldiers fight without conviction and lose their determination.

The political goal must be clearly and precisely indicated to inhabitants of guerrilla zones and their national consciousness awakened. Hence, a concrete explanation of the political systems used is important not only to guerrilla troops but to all those who are concerned with the realization of our political goal. The Kuomintang has issued a pamphlet entitled

*System of National Organization for War,* which should be widely distributed throughout guerrilla zones. If we lack national organization, we will lack the essential unity that should exist between the soldiers and the people.

A study and comprehension of the political objectives of this war and of the anti-Japanese front is particularly important for officers of guerrilla troops. There are some militarists who say: 'We are not interested in politics but only in the profession of arms.' It is vital that these simple-minded militarists be made to realize the relationship that exists between politics and military affairs. Military action is a method used to attain a political goal. While military affairs and political affairs are not identical, it is impossible to isolate one from the other.

It is to be hoped that the world is in the last era of strife. The vast majority of human beings have already prepared or are preparing to fight a war that will bring justice to the oppressed peopled of the world. No matter how long this war may last, there is no doubt that it will be followed by an unprecedented epoch of peace The war that we are fighting today for the freedom of all human beings, and the independent, happy, and liberal China that we are fighting to establish will be a part of that new world order. A conception like this is difficult for the simple-minded militarist to grasp and it must therefore be carefully explained to him.

There are three additional matters that must be considered under the broad question of political activities. These are political activities, first, as applied to the troops; second, as applied to the people; and, third, as applied to the enemy. The fundamental problems are: first, spiritual unification of officers and men within the army; second spiritual unification of the army and the people; of the army and the people; and, last, destruction of the unity of the enemy. The concrete methods for achieving these unities are discussed in detail in pamphlet Number 4 of this series, entitled *Political Activities in Anti-Japanese Guerrilla Warfare.*

A revolutionary army must have discipline that is established on a limited democratic basis. In all armies, obedience the subordinates to their superiors must be exacted. This is true in the case of guerrilla discipline, but the basis for guerrilla discipline must be the individual conscience. With guerrillas, a discipline of compulsion is ineffective. In any revolutionary army, there is unity of purpose as far as both officers and men are concerned, and, therefore, within such an army, discipline is self-imposed. Although discipline in guerrilla ranks is not as severe as in the ranks of orthodox forces, the necessity for discipline exists. This must be self-imposed, because only when it is, is the soldier able to understand completely, why he fights and why he must obey. This type of discipline becomes a tower of strength within the army, and it is the only type that can truly harmonize the relationship that exists between officers and soldiers.

In any system where discipline is externally imposed, the relationship that exists between officer and man is characterized by indifference of the one to the other. The idea that officers can physically beat or severely tongue-lash their men is a feudal one and is not in accord with the conception of self-imposed discipline. Discipline of the feudal type will destroy internal unity and fighting strength. A discipline self-imposed is the primary characteristic of a democratic system in the army.

A secondary characteristic is found in the degree of liberties accorded officers and soldiers. In a revolutionary army, all individuals enjoy political liberty and the question, for example, of the emancipation of the people must not only be tolerated but discussed, and propaganda must be encouraged. Further, in such an army, the mode of living of the officers and the soldiers must not differ too much, and this is particularly true in the case of guerilla troops. Officers should live under the same conditions as their men, for that is the only way in which they can gain from their men the admiration and confidence so vital in war. It is incorrect to hold to a theory of equality in all things. But there must be equality of existence in accepting the hardships and dangers of war, thus we may attain to the unification of the officer and soldier groups a unity both horizontal within the group itself, and vertical, that is, from lower to higher echelons. It is only when such unity is present that units can be said to be powerful combat factors.

There is also a unity of spirit that should exist between troops and local inhabitants. The Eighth Route Army put into practice a code known as 'Three Rules and the Eight Remarks', which we list here:

Rules:

All actions are subject to command.
Do not steal from the people.
Be neither selfish nor unjust.

Remarks:

Replace the door when you leave the house.
Roll up the bedding on which you have slept.
Be courteous.
Be honest in your transactions.
Return what you borrow.
Replace what you break.

Do not bathe in the presence of women.
Do not without authority search those you arrest.

The Red Army adhered to this code for ten years and the Eighth Route Army and other units have since adopted it.

Many people think it impossible for guerrillas to exist for long in the enemy's rear. Such a belief reveals lack of comprehension of the relationship that should exist between the people and the troops. The former may be likened to water the latter to the fish which inhabit it. How may it be said that these two cannot exist together? It is only undisciplined troops who make the people their enemies and who, like the fish out of its native element cannot live.

We further our mission of destroying the enemy by propagandizing his troops, by treating his captured soldiers with consideration, and by caring for those of his wounded who fall into our hands. If we fail in these respects, we strengthen the solidarity of our enemy.

# CHAPTER 7

## The Strategy of Guerrilla Resistance against Japan

It has been definitely decided that in the strategy of our war against Japan, guerrilla strategy must be auxiliary to fundamental orthodox methods. If this were a small country, guerrilla activities could be carried out close to the scene of operations of the regular army and directly complementary to them. In such a case, there would be no question of guerrilla strategy as such. Nor would the question arise if our country were as strong as Russia, for example, and able speedily to eject an invader. The question exists because China, a weak country of vast size, has today progressed to the point where it has become possible to adopt the policy of a protracted war characterized by guerrilla operations. Although these may at first glance seem to be abnormal or heterodox, such is not actually the case.

Because Japanese military power is inadequate, much of the territory her armies have overrun is without sufficient garrison troops. Under such circumstances the primary functions of guerrillas are three: first, to conduct a war on exterior lines, that is, in the rear of the enemy; second, to establish bases, and, last, to extend the war areas. Thus, guerrilla participation in the war is not merely a matter of purely local guerrilla tactics but involves strategic considerations.

Such war, with its vast time and space factors, establishes a new military process, the focal point of which is China today. The Japanese are apparently attempting to recall a past that saw the Yuan extinguish the Sung and the Ch'ing conquer the Ming; that witnessed the extension of the British Empire to North America and India; that saw the Latins overrun Central and South America. As far as China today is concerned, such dreams of conquest are fantastic and without reality. Today's China is better equipped than was the China of yesterday, and a new type of guerrilla hostilities is a part of that equipment. If our enemy fails to take these facts into consideration and makes too optimistic an estimate of the situation, he courts disaster.

Though the strategy of guerrillas is inseparable from war strategy as a whole, the actual conduct of these hostilities differs from the conduct of orthodox operations. Each type of warfare has methods peculiar to itself, and methods suitable to regular warfare cannot be applied with success to the special situations that confront guerrillas.

Before we treat the practical aspects of guerrilla war, it might be well to recall the fundamental axiom of combat on which all military action is based. This can be stated: 'Conservation of one's own strength; destruction of enemy strength.' A military policy based on this axiom is consonant with a national policy directed towards the building of a free and prosperous Chinese state and the destruction of Japanese imperialism. It is in furtherance of this policy that government applies in military strength. Is the sacrifice demanded by war in conflict with the idea of self-preservation? Not at all. The sacrifices demanded are necessary both to destroy the enemy and to preserve ourselves; the sacrifice of a part of the people is necessary to preserve the whole. All the considerations of military action are derived from this axiom. Its application is as apparent in all tactical and strategic conceptions as it is in the simple case of the soldier who shoots at his enemy from a covered position.

All guerrilla units start from nothing and grow. What methods should we select to ensure the conservation and development of our own strength and the destruction of that of the enemy? The essential requirements are the six listed below:

1. Retention of the initiative; alertness; carefully planned tactical attacks in a war of strategic defense; tactical speed in a war strategically protracted, tactical operations on exterior lines in a war conducts strategically on interior lines.
2. Conduct of operations to complement those of the regular army.
3. The establishment of bases.
4. A clear understanding of the relationship that exists between the attack and the defense.
5. The development of mobile operations.
6. Correct command.

The enemy, though numerically weak, is strong in the quality of his troops and their equipment; we, on the other hand, are strong numerically but weak as to quality. These considerations have been taken into account in the development of the policy of tactical offence, tactical speed, and tactical operations on exterior lines in a war that, strategically speaking, is defensive in character, protracted in nature, and conducted along interior lines. Our strategy is based on these conceptions. They must be kept in mind in the conduct of all operations.

Although the element of surprise is not absent in orthodox warfare, there are fewer opportunities to apply it than there are during guerrilla hostilities. In the latter, speed is essential. The movements of guerrilla troops must be secret and of supernatural rapidity; the enemy must be taken unaware, and the action entered speedily. There can be no procrastination in the execution of plans; no assumption of a negative or passive defense; no great dispersion of forces in many local engagements. The basic method is the attack in a violent and deceptive form.

While there may be cases where the attack will extend over a period of several days (if that length of time in necessary to annihilate an enemy group), it is more profitable to launch and push an attack with maximum speed. The tactics of defense have no place in the realm of guerrilla warfare. If a delaying action is necessary, such places as defiles, river crossings, and villages offer the most suitable conditions, for it is in such places that the enemy's arrangements may be disrupted and he may be annihilated.

The enemy is much stronger than we are, and it is true that we can hinder, distract, disperse, and destroy him only if we disperse our own forces. Although guerrilla warfare is the warfare of such dispersed units, it is sometimes desirable to concentrate in order to destroy an enemy. Thus, the principle of concentration of force against a relatively weaker enemy is applicable to guerrilla warfare.

We can prolong this struggle and make of it a protracted war only by gaining positive and lightning-like tactical decisions; by employing our manpower in proper concentrations and dispersions; and by operation on exterior lines in order to surround and destroy our enemy. If we cannot surround whole armies, we can at least partially destroy them, if we cannot kill the Japanese, we can capture them. The total effect of many local successes will be to change the relative strengths of the opposing forces. The destruction of Japan's military power, combined with the international sympathy for China's cause and the revolutionary tendencies evident in Japan, will be sufficient to destroy Japanese imperialism.

*Mao Zedong*

We will next discuss initiative, alertness, and the matter of careful planning. What is meant by initiative in warfare? In all battles and wars, a struggle to gain and retain the initiative goes on between the opposing sides, for it is the side that holds the initiative that has liberty of action. When an army loses the initiative, it loses its liberty; its role becomes passive; it faces the danger of defeat and destruction.

It is more difficult to obtain the initiative when defending on interior lines than it is while attacking on exterior lines. This is what Japan is doing. There are, however, several weak points as far as Japan is concerned. One of these is lack of sufficient manpower for the task; another is her cruelty to the inhabitants of conquered areas; a third is the underestimation of Chinese strength, which has resulted in the differences between military cliques, which, in turn, have been productive of many mistakes in the direction of her military forces. For instance, she has been gradually compelled to increase her manpower in China while, at the same time, the many arguments over plans of operations and disposition of troops have resulted in the loss of good opportunities for improvement of her strategic position.

This explains the fact that although the Japanese are frequently able to surround large bodies of Chinese troops, they have never yet been able to capture more than a few. The Japanese military machine is thus being weakened by insufficiency of manpower, inadequacy of resources, the barbarism of her troops, and the general stupidity that has characterized the conduct of operations. Her offensive continues unabated, but because of the weaknesses pointed out, her attack must be limited in extent. She can never conquer China. The day will come — indeed already has in some areas — when she will be forced into a passive role. When hostilities commenced, China was passive, but as we enter the second phase of the war we find ourselves pursuing a strategy of mobile warfare, with both guerrillas and regulars operating on exterior lines. Thus, with each passing day, we seize some degree of initiative from the Japanese.

The matter of initiative is especially serious for guerrilla forces; who must face critical situations unknown to regular troops. The superiority of the enemy and the lack of unity and experience within our own ranks may be cited. Guerrillas can, however, gain the initiative if they keep in mind the weak points of the enemy. Because of the enemy's insufficient manpower, guerrillas can operate over vast territories, because he is a foreigner and a barbarian, guerrillas can gain the confidence of millions of their countrymen; because of the stupidity of enemy commanders, guerrillas can make full use of their own cleverness. Both guerrillas and regulars must exploit these enemy weaknesses while, at the same time, our own are remedied. Some of our weaknesses are apparent only and are, in actuality, sources of strength. For example, the very fact that most guerrilla groups are small makes it desirable and advantageous for them to appear and disappear in the enemy's rear. With such activities, the enemy is simply unable to cope. A similar liberty of action can rarely be obtained by regular forces.

When the enemy attacks the guerrillas with more than one column, it is difficult for the latter to retain the initiative. Any error, no matter how slight, in the estimation of the situation is likely to result in forcing the guerrillas into a passive role. They will then find themselves unable to fend off the attacks of the enemy.

It is apparent that we can gain and retain the initiative only by a correct estimation of the situation and a proper arrangement of all military and political factors. A too pessimistic estimate will operate to force us into a passive position, with consequent loss of initiative; an overly optimistic estimate, with its rash ordering of factors, will produce the same result.

No military leader is endowed by heaven with an ability to seize the initiative. It is the intelligent leader who does so after a careful study and estimate of the situation and arrangement of the military and political factors involved. When a guerrilla unit, through either a poor estimate on the part of its leader or pressure from the enemy, is forced into a passive position, its first duty is to extricate itself. No method can be prescribed for this, as the method to be employed will, in every case, depend on the situation. One can, if necessary, run away. But there are times when the situation seems hopeless and, in reality, is not so at all. It is at such times that the good leader recognizes and seizes the moment when he can regain the lost initiative.

Let us revert to alertness. To conduct one's troops with alertness is an essential of guerrilla command. Leaders must realize that to operate alertly is the most important factor in gaining the initiative and vital in its effect of the relative situation that exists between our forces and those of the enemy. Guerrilla commanders adjust their operations to the enemy situation, to the terrain, and to prevailing local conditions. Leaders must be alert to sense changes in these factors and make necessary modifications in troop dispositions to accord with them. The leader must be like a fisherman, who, with his nets, is able both to cast them and to pull them out in awareness of the depth of the water, the strength of the current or the presence of any obstructions that may foul them. As the fisherman controls his nets through the lead ropes, so the guerrilla leader maintains contact with control over his units. As the fisherman must change his position, so must the guerrilla commander. Dispersion, concentration, constant change of position—it is in these ways that guerrillas employ, their strength.

In general, guerrilla units disperse to operate:

1. When the enemy is in over-extended defense, and sufficient force cannot be concentrated against him, guerrillas must disperse, harass him, and demoralize him.
2. When encircled by the enemy, guerrillas disperse to withdraw.
3. When the nature of the ground limits action, guerrillas disperse.
4. When the availability of supplies limits action, they disperse.
5. Guerrillas disperse in order to promote mass movements over a wide area.

Regardless of the circumstances that prevail at the time of dispersal, caution must be exercised in certain matters:

A relatively large group should be retained as a central force. The remainder of the troops should not be divided into groups of absolutely equal size. In this way, the leader is in a position to deal with any circumstances that may arise. Each dispersed unit should have clear and definite responsibilities. Orders should specify a place to which to proceed, the time of proceeding, and the place, time, and method of assembly.

Guerrillas concentrate when the enemy is advancing upon them, and there is opportunity to fall upon him and destroy him. Concentration may be desirable when the enemy is on the defensive and guerrillas wish to destroy isolated detachments in particular localities. By the term 'concentrate', we do not mean the assembly of all manpower but rather of only that necessary for the task. The remaining guerrillas are assigned missions of hindering and delaying the enemy, of destroys isolated groups, or of conducting mass propaganda.

In addition to the dispersion and concentration of forces, the leader must understand what is termed 'alert shifting'. When the enemy feels the danger of guerrillas, he will generally send troops out to attack them. The guerrillas must consider the situation and decide at what time and at what place they wish to fight. If they find that they cannot fight, they must immediately shift. Then the enemy may be destroyed piecemeal. For example; after a guerrilla group has destroyed an enemy detachment at one place, it may be shifted to another area to attack and destroy a second detachment. Sometimes, it will not be profitable for a unit to become engaged in a certain area, and in that case, it must move immediately.

When the situation is serious, the guerrilla must move with the fluidity of water and the ease of the blowing wind. Their tactics must deceive, tempt, and confuse the enemy. They must lead the enemy to believe that they will attack him from the east and north, and they must then strike him from the west and the south. They must strike, then rapidly disperse. They must move at night.

Guerrilla initiative is expressed in dispersion, concentration, and the alert shifting of forces. If guerrillas are stupid and obstinate, they will be led to passive positions and severely damaged. Skill in conducting guerrilla operations, however, lies not in merely understanding the things we have discussed but rather in their actual application on the field of battle. The quick intelligence that constantly watches the ever-changing situation and is able to seize on the right moment for decisive action is found only in keen and thoughtful observers.

Careful planning is necessary if victory is to be won in guerrilla war, and those who fight without method do not understand the nature of guerrilla action. A plan is necessary regardless of the size of the unit involved; a prudent plan is as necessary in the case of the squad as in the case of the regiment. The situation must be carefully studied, then an assignment of duties made. Plans must include both political and military instruction; the matter of supply and equipment, and the matter of co-operation with local civilians. Without study of these factors, it is impossible either to seize the initiative or to operate alertly. It is true that guerrillas can make only limited plans, but even so, the factors we have mentioned must be considered.

The initiative can be secured and retained only following a positive victory that results from attack. The attack must be made on guerrilla initiative; that is, guerrillas must not permit themselves to be maneuvered into a position where they are robbed of initiative and where the decision to attack is forced upon them. Any victory will result from careful planning and alert control. Even in defense, all our efforts must be directed toward a resumption of the attack, for it is only by attack that we can extinguish our enemies and preserve ourselves. A defense or a withdrawal is entirely useless as far as extinguishing our enemies is concerned and of only temporary value, as far as the conservation of our forces is concerned. This principle is valid both for guerrillas and regular troops. The differences are of degree only; that is to say, in the manner of execution.

The relationship that exists between guerrilla and the orthodox forces is important and must be appreciated. Generally speaking, there are types of co-operation between guerrillas and orthodox groups. These are:

1. Strategic co-operation
2. Tactical co-operation
3. Battle co-operation

Guerrillas who harass the enemy's rear installations and hinder his transport are weakening him and encouraging the national spirit of resistance. They are co-operating strategically. For example, the guerrillas in Manchuria had no functions of strategic co-operation with orthodox forces until the war in China started. Since that time, their faction of strategic co-operation is evident, for if they can kill one enemy, make the enemy expend one round of ammunition, or hinder one enemy group in its advance southward, our powers of resistance here are proportionately increased. Such guerrilla action has a positive action on the enemy nation and on its troops, while, at the same time, it encourages our own countrymen. Another example of strategic co-operation is furnished by the guerrillas who operate along the P'ing-Sui, P'ing-Han, Chin-P'u, T'ung-Pu, and Cheng-T'ai railways. This co-operation began when the invader attacked, continued during the period when he held garrisoned cities in the areas, and was intensified when our regular forces counter-attacked, in an effort to restore the lost territories.

As an example of tactical co-operation, we may cite the operations at Hsing-K'ou, when guerrillas both north and south of Yeh Men destroyed the T'ung-P'u railway and the motor roads near P'ing Hosing Pass and Yang Fang K'ou. A number of small operating base were established, and organized guerrilla action in Shansi complemented the activities of the regular forces both there and in the defense of Honan. similarly, during the south Shantung campaign, guerrillas in the five northern provinces co-operated with the army's operation on the Hsuchow front.

Guerrilla commanders in rear areas and those in command of regiments assigned to operate with orthodox units must co-operate in accordance with the situation. It is their function to determine weak points in the enemy dispositions, harass them, to disrupt their transport, and to undermine their morale, If guerrilla action were independent, the results to be obtained from tactical co-operation would be lost and those that result from strategic co-operation greatly diminished. In order to accomplish their mission and improve the degree of co-operation, guerrilla units must be equipped with some means of rapid communication. For this purpose, two way radio sets are recommended.

Guerrilla forces in the immediate battle area are responsible for close co-operation with regular forces, Their principal functions are to hinder enemy transport to gather information, and to act as outposts and sentinels. Even without precise instructions from the commander of the regular forces, these missions, as well as any others that contribute to the general success, should be assumed.

The problem of establishment of bases is of particular importance. This is so because this war is a cruel and protracted struggle. The lost territories can be restored only by a strategic counter-attack and this we cannot carry out until the enemy is well into China. Consequently, some part of our country — or, indeed, most of it — may be captured by the enemy and become his rear area. It is our task to develop intensive guerrilla warfare over this vast area and convert the enemy's rear into an additional front. Thus the enemy will never be able to stop fighting. In order to subdue the occupied territory, the enemy will have to become increasingly severe and oppressive.

A guerrilla base may be defined as an area, strategically located, in which the guerrillas can carry out their duties of training, self-preservation and development. Ability to fight a war without a rear area is a fundamental characteristic of guerrilla action, but this does not mean that guerrilla can exist and function over a long period of time without the development of base areas. History shows us many examples of peasant revolts that were unsuccessful, and it is fanciful to believe that such movements, characterized by banditry and brigandage, could succeed in this era of improved communications and military equipment. Some guerrilla leaders seem to think that those qualities are present in today's movement, and before such leaders can comprehend the importance of base areas in the long-term war, their mind must be disabused of this idea.

The subject of bases may be better understood if we consider:

1. The various categories of bases
2. Guerrilla areas and base areas
3. The establishment of bases
4. The development of bases

Guerrilla bases may be classified according to their location as: first, mountain bases; second, plains bases; and last, river, lake, and bay bases. The advantages of bases in mountainous areas are evident. Those which are now established are at Ch'ang P'o Chan, Wu Tai Shan, Taiheng Shan, Tai Shan, Yen Shan, and Mao Shan. These bases are strongly protected. Similar bases should be established in all enemy rear areas.

Plains country is generally not satisfactory for guerrilla operating bases, but this does not mean that guerrilla warfare cannot flourish in such country or that bases cannot be established there. The extent of guerrilla development in Hopeh and west Shantung proves the opposite to be the case. Whether we can count on the use of these bases over long periods of time is questionable. We can, however, establish small bases of a seasonal or temporary nature. This we can do because our barbaric enemy simply does not have the manpower to occupy all the areas he has overrun and because the population of China is so numerous that a base can be established anywhere. Seasonal bases in plains country may be established in the winter when the rivers are frozen over, and in the summer when the crops are growing. Temporary bases may be established when the enemy is otherwise occupied. When the enemy advances, the guerrillas who have established bases in the plains area are the first to engage him. Upon their withdrawal into mountainous country, they should leave behind them guerrilla groups dispersed over the entire area. Guerrillas shift from base to base on the theory that they must be in one place one day and another place the next.

There are many historical examples of the establishment of bases in river, bay, and lake country, and this is one aspect of our activity that has so far received little attention. Red guerrillas held out for many years in the Hungtze Lake region. We should establish bases in the Hungtze and Tai areas and along rivers and watercourses in territory controlled by the enemy so as to deny him access to, and free use of, the water routes.

There is a difference between the terms base area and guerrilla area. An area completely surrounded by territory occupied by the enemy is a 'base area'. Wu Tai Shan, and Taiheng Shan are examples of base areas. On the other hand, the area east and north of Wu Tai Shan (the Shansi-Hopeh-Chahar border zone) is a guerrilla area. Such areas can be controlled by guerrillas only while they actually physically occupy them. Upon their departure, control reverts to a puppet pro-Japanese government. East Hopeh, for example, was at first a guerrilla area rather than a base area. A puppet government functioned there. Eventually, the people, organized and inspired by guerrillas from the Wu Tai mountains, assisted in the transformation of this guerrilla area into a real base area. Such a task is extremely difficult, for it is largely dependent upon the degree to which the people can be inspired. In certain garrisoned areas, such as the cities and zones contiguous to the railways, the guerrillas see unable to drive the Japanese and puppets out. These areas remain guerrilla areas. At other times, base areas might become guerrilla areas due either to our own mistakes or to the activities of the enemy.

Obviously, in any given area in the war zone, any one or three situations may develop: The area may remain in Chinese hands; it may be lost to the Japanese and puppets or it may be divided between the combatants. Guerrilla leaders should endeavor to see that either the first or the last of these situations is assured.

Another point essential in the establishment of bases is the co-operation that must exist between the armed guerrilla bands and the people. All our strength must be used to spread the doctrine of armed resistance to Japan, to arm the people, to organize self-defense units, and to train guerrilla bands. This doctrine must be spread among the people, who must be organized into anti-Japanese groups. Their political instincts must be sharpened and their martial ardor increased. If the workers, the farmers, the lovers of liberty, the young men, the women, and the children are not organized, they will never realize their own anti-Japanese power. Only the united strength of the people can eliminate traitors, recover the measure of political power that has been lost, and conserve and improve what we still retain.

We have already touched on geographic factors in our discussion of bases, and we must also mention the economic aspects of the problem. What economic policy should be adopted? Any such policy must offer reasonable protection to commerce and business. We interpret 'reasonable protection' to mean the people must contribute money in proportion to the money they have. Farmers will be required to furnish a certain share of their crops to guerrilla troops. Confiscation, except in the case of business run by traitors, is prohibited.

Our activities must be extended over the entire periphery of the base area if we wish to attack the enemy's bases and thus strengthen and develop our own. This will afford us opportunity to organize, equip, and train the people, thus furthering guerrilla policy as well as the national policy of protected war. At times, we must emphasize the development and extension of base areas; at other times, the organization, training, or equipment of the people.

Each guerrilla base will have its own peculiar problems of attack and defense. In general, the enemy, in an endeavor to consolidate his gains, will attempt to extinguish guerrilla bases by dispatching numerous bodies of troops over a number of different routes. This must be anticipated and the encirclement broken by counter-attacks As such enemy columns are without reserves, we should plan on using our main forces to attack one of them by surprise and devote our secondary effort to continual hindrance and harassment. At the same time, other forces should isolate enemy garrison troops and operate on their lines of supply and communication. When one column has been disposed of, we may turn our attention to one of the others. In a base area as large as Wu Tat Shan, for example, there are four or five military sub-divisions. Guerrillas in these sub-divisions must co-operate to form a primary force to counterattack the enemy, or the area from which he came, while a secondary force harasses and hinders him.

After defeating the enemy in any area, we must take advantage of the period he requires for reorganization to press home our attacks. We must not attack an objective we are not certain of winning. We must confine our operations to relatively small areas and destroy the enemy and traitors in those places.

When the inhabitants have been inspired, new volunteers accepted trained, equipped, and organized, our operations may be extended to include cities and lines of communication not strongly held. We may hold these at least for temporary (if not permanent) periods. All these are our duties in offensive strategy. Their object is to lengthen the period that the enemy must remain on the defensive. Then our military activities and our organization work among the masses of the people must be zealously expanded; and with equal zeal, the strength of the enemy attacked and diminished. It is of great importance that guerrilla units be rested and instructed. During such times as the enemy is on the defensive, the troops may get some rest and instruction may be carried out.

The development of mobile warfare is not only possible but essential. This is the case because our current war is a desperate and protracted struggle. If China were able to conquer the Japanese bandits speedily and to recover her lost territories, there would be no question of long-term war on a national scale. Hence there would no question of the relation of guerrilla hostilities into mobile warfare of an orthodox nature; both the quantity and quality of guerrilla must be improved. Primarily, more men must join the armies; then the quality of equipment and standards of training must be improved. Political training must be emphasized and our organization, the technique of handling our weapons, our tactics — all must be improved. Our internal discipline must be strengthened. The soldiers must be educated politically. There must be a gradual change from guerrilla formations to orthodox regimental organization. The necessary bureaus and staffs, both political and military, must be provided. At the same time, attention must be paid to the creation of suitable supply, medical, and hygiene units. The standards of equipment must be raised and types of weapons increased. Communication equipment must not be forgotten. Orthodox standards of discipline must be established.

Because guerrilla formations act independently and because they are the most elementary of armed formations, command cannot be too highly centralized. If it were, guerilla action would be too limited in scope. At the same time, guerrilla activities, to be most effective, must be co-ordinated, not only in so far as they themselves are concerned, but additionally with regular troops operating in the same areas. This co-ordination is a function of the war zone commander and his staff.

In guerrilla base areas, the command must be centralized for strategic purposes and decentralized for tactical purposes. Centralized strategic command takes care of the general management of all guerrilla units, their co-ordination within war zones, and the general policy regarding guerrilla base areas. Beyond this, centralization of command will result in interference with subordinate units, as, naturally, the tactics to apply to concrete situations can be determined only as these various situations arise. This is true in orthodox warfare when communications between lower and higher echelons break down. In a word, proper guerrilla policy will provide for unified strategy and independent activity.

Each guerrilla area is divided into districts and these in turn are divided into sub-districts. Each sub-division has its appointed commander, and while general plans are made by higher commanders, the nature of actions is determined by inferior commanders. The former may suggest the nature of the action to be taken but cannot define it. Thus inferior groups heave more or less complete local control.

# COLLECTED WRITINGS OF CHAIRMAN MAO

Volume 2

# GUERRILLA WARFARE

## PART 2

# PROBLEMS OF STRATEGY IN GUERRILLA WAR AGAINST JAPAN

## Preface

### May, 1938

In the early days of the War of Resistance against Japan, many people inside and outside the Party belittled the important strategic role of guerrilla warfare and pinned their hopes on regular warfare alone, and particularly on the operations of the Kuomintang forces. Comrade Mao Zedong refuted this view and wrote this article to show the correct road of development for anti Japanese guerrilla warfare.

As a result, the Eighth Route Army and the New Fourth Army, which had just over 40,000 men when the War of Resistance began in 1937, grew to a great army of one million by the time Japan surrendered in 1945, established many revolutionary base areas, played a great part in the war and thus, throughout this period, made Chiang Kai-shek afraid to capitulate to Japan or launch a nation-wide civil war.

In 1946, when Chiang Kai-shek did launch a nation-wide civil war, the People's Liberation Army, formed out of the Eighth Route and New Fourth Armies, was strong enough to deal with his attacks.

*Mao Zedong*

# CHAPTER 1

# Why Raise the Question of Strategy?

In the War of Resistance against Japan, regular warfare is primary and guerrilla warfare supplementary. This point has already been correctly settled. Thus, it seems there are only tactical problems in guerrilla warfare. Why then raise the question of strategy?

If China were a small country in which the role of guerrilla warfare was only to render direct support over short distances to the campaigns of the regular army, there would, of course, be only tactical problems but no strategic ones. On the other hand, if China were a country as strong as the Soviet Union and the invading enemy could either be quickly expelled, or, even though his expulsion were to take some time, he could not occupy extensive areas, then again guerrilla warfare would simply play a supporting role in campaigns, and would naturally involve only tactical but not strategic problems.

The question of strategy in guerrilla war does arise, however, in the case of China, which is neither small nor like the Soviet Union, but which is both a large and a weak country. This large and weak country is being attacked by a small and strong country, but the large and weak country is in an era of progress; this is the source of the whole problem. It is in these circumstances that vast areas have come under enemy occupation and that the war has become a protracted one. The enemy is occupying vast areas of this large country of ours, but Japan is a small country, she does not have sufficient soldiers and has to leave many gaps in the occupied areas, so that our anti Japanese guerrilla warfare consists primarily not in interior-line operations in support of the campaigns of the regular troops but in independent operations on exterior lines; furthermore, China is progressive, that is to say, she has a staunch army and broad masses of people, both led by the Communist Party, so that, far from being small-scale, our anti-Japanese guerrilla warfare is in fact large-scale warfare. Hence the emergence of a whole series of problems, such as the strategic defensive, the strategic offensive, etc. The protracted nature of the war and its attendant ruthlessness have made it imperative for guerrilla warfare to undertake many unusual tasks; hence such problems as those of the base areas, the development of guerrilla warfare into mobile warfare, and so on. For all these reasons, China's guerrilla warfare against Japan has broken out of the bounds of tactics to knock at the gates of strategy, and it demands examination from the viewpoint of strategy. The point that merits our particular attention is that such extensive as well as protracted guerrilla warfare is quite new in the entire history of war. This is bound up with the fact that we are now in the Nineteen Thirties and Nineteen Forties and that we now have the Communist Party and the Red Army. Herein lies the heart of the matter. Our enemy is probably still cherishing fond dreams of emulating the Mongol conquest of the Sung Dynasty, the Manchu conquest of the Ming Dynasty, the British occupation of North America and India, the Latin occupation of Central and South America, etc. But such dreams have no practical value in present-day China because there are certain factors present in the China of today which were absent in those historical instances, and one of them is guerrilla warfare, which is quite a new phenomenon. If our enemy overlooks this fact, he will certainly come to grief.

These are the reasons why our anti-Japanese guerrilla warfare, though occupying only a supplementary place in the

War of Resistance as a whole, must nevertheless be examined from the viewpoint of strategy.

Why not, then, apply to guerrilla warfare the general strategic principles of the War of Resistance?

The question of strategy in our anti-Japanese guerrilla warfare is indeed closely linked with the question of strategy in the War of Resistance as a whole, because they have much in common. On the other hand, guerrilla warfare is different from regular warfare and has its own peculiarities, and consequently many peculiar elements are involved in the question of strategy in guerrilla warfare. With out modification it is impossible to apply the strategic principles of the War of Resistance in general to guerrilla warfare with its own peculiarities.

# CHAPTER 2

## The Basic Principle of War is to Preserve Oneself and Destroy the Enemy

Before discussing the question of strategy in guerrilla warfare in concrete terms, a few words are needed on the fundamental problem of war. All the guiding principles of military operations grow out of the one basic principle: to strive to the utmost to preserve one's own strength and destroy that of the enemy. In a revolutionary war, this principle is directly linked with basic political principles. For instance, the basic political principle of China's War of Resistance against Japan, i.e., its political aim, is to drive out Japanese imperialism and build an independent, free and happy new China.

In terms of military action this principle means the use of armed force to defend our motherland and to drive out the Japanese invaders. To attain this end, the operations of the armed units take the form of doing their utmost to preserve their own strength on the one hand and destroy the enemy's on the other. How then do we justify the encouragement of heroic sacrifice in war? Every war exacts a price, sometimes an extremely high one. Is this not in contradiction with "preserving oneself"? In fact, there is no contradiction at all; to put it more exactly, sacrifice and self-preservation are both opposite and complementary to each other. For such sacrifice is essential not only for destroying the enemy but also for preserving oneself -- partial and temporary "non-preservation" (sacrifice, or paying the price) is necessary for the sake of general and permanent preservation. From this basic principle stems the series of principles guiding military operations, all of which -- from the principles of shooting (taking cover to preserve oneself, and making full use of fire-power to destroy the enemy) to the principles of strategy -- are permeated with the spirit of this basic principle. All technical, tactical and strategic principles represent applications of this basic principle. The principle of preserving one self and destroying the enemy is the basis of all military principles.

CHAPTER 3

# Six Specific Problems of Strategy in Guerrilla War against Japan

Now let us see what policies or principles have to be adopted in guerrilla operations against Japan before we can attain the object of preserving ourselves and destroying the enemy. Since the guerrilla units in the War of Resistance (and in all other revolutionary wars) generally grow out of nothing and expand from a small to a large force, they must preserve themselves and, moreover, they must expand. Hence the question is, what policies or principles have to be adopted before we can attain the object of preserving and expanding ourselves and destroying the enemy?

Generally speaking, the main principles are as follows: (1) the use of initiative, flexibility and planning in conducting offensives within the defensive, battles of quick decision within protracted war, and exterior-line operations within interior-line operations; (2) co-ordination with regular warfare; (3) establishment of base areas; (4) the strategic defensive and the strategic offensive; (5) the development of guerrilla warfare into mobile warfare; and (6) correct relationship of command. These six items constitute the whole of the strategic program for guerrilla war against Japan and are the means necessary for the preservation and expansion of our forces, for the destruction and expulsion of the enemy, for co-ordination with regular warfare and the winning of final victory.

# CHAPTER 4

## Initiative, Flexibility and Planning in Conducting Offensives within the Defensive Battles of Quick Decision within Protracted War, and Exterior-Line Operations within Interior-Line Operations

Here the subject may be dealt with under four headings: (1) the relationship between the defensive and the offensive, between protractedness and quick decision, and between the interior and exterior lines; (2) the initiative in all operations; (3) flexible employment of forces; and (4) planning in all operations.

To start with the first.

If we take the War of Resistance as a whole, the fact that Japan is a strong country and is attacking while China is a weak country and is defending herself makes our war strategically a defensive and protracted war. As far as the operational lines are concerned, the Japanese are operating on exterior and we on interior lines. This is one aspect of the situation. But there is another aspect which is just the reverse. The enemy forces, though strong (in arms, in certain qualities of their men, and certain other factors), are numerically small, whereas our forces, though weak (likewise, in arms, in certain qualities of our men, and certain other factors), are numerically very large. Added to the fact that the enemy is an alien nation invading our country while we are resisting his invasion on our own soil, this determines the following strategy. It is possible and necessary to use tactical offensives within the strategic defensive, to fight campaigns and battles of quick decision within a strategically protracted war and to fight campaigns and battles on exterior lines within strategically interior lines. Such is the strategy to be adopted in the War of Resistance as a whole. It holds true both for regular and for guerrilla warfare. Guerrilla warfare is different only in degree and form. Offensives in guerrilla warfare generally take the form of surprise attacks. Although surprise attacks can and should be employed in regular warfare too, the degree of surprise is less. In guerrilla warfare, the need to bring operations to a quick decision is very great, and our exterior-line ring of encirclement of the enemy in campaigns and battles is very small All these distinguish it from regular warfare.

Thus it can be seen that in their operations guerrilla units have to concentrate the maximum forces, act secretly and swiftly, attack the enemy by surprise and bring battles to a quick decision, and that they must strictly avoid passive defense, procrastination and the dispersal of forces before engagements. Of course, guerrilla warfare includes not only the strategic but also the tactical defensive. The latter embraces, among other things, containing and outpost actions during battles; the disposition of forces for resistance at narrow passes, strategic points, rivers or villages in order to deplete and exhaust the enemy; and action to cover withdrawal. But the basic principle of guerrilla warfare must be the offensive, and guerrilla warfare is more offensive in its character than regular warfare. The offensive, moreover, must take the form of surprise attacks, and to expose our selves by ostentatiously parading our forces is even less permissible in guerrilla warfare than in regular warfare. From the fact that the enemy is strong and we are weak it necessarily follows that, in guerrilla operations in general even more than in regular warfare, battles must be decided quickly, though on some occasions guerrilla fighting may be kept up for several days, as in an assault on a small and isolated enemy force cut off from help. Because of its dispersed character, guerrilla warfare can spread everywhere, and in many of its tasks, as in harassing, containing and disrupting the enemy and in mass work, its principle is dispersal of forces; but a guerrilla unit, or a guerrilla formation, must concentrate its main forces when it is engaged in destroying the enemy, and especially when it is striving to smash an enemy attack. "Concentrate a big force to strike at a small section of the enemy force" remains a principle of field operations in guerrilla warfare.

Thus it can also be seen that, if we take the War of Resistance as a whole, we can attain the aim of our strategic defensive and finally defeat Japanese imperialism only through the cumulative effect of many offensive campaigns and battles in both regular and guerrilla warfare, namely, through the cumulative effect of many victories in offensive actions. Only through the cumulative effect of many campaigns and battles of quick decision, namely, the cumulative effect of many victories achieved through quick decision in offensive campaigns and battles, can we attain our goal of strategic protractedness, which means gaining time to increase our capacity to resist while hastening or awaiting changes in the international situation and the internal collapse of the enemy, in order to be able to launch a strategic counter-offensive and drive the Japanese invaders out of China. We must concentrate superior forces and fight exterior-line operations in every campaign or battle, whether in the stage of strategic defensive or in that of strategic counter-offensive, in order to encircle and destroy the enemy forces, encircling part if not all of them, destroying part if not all of the forces we have encircled, and inflicting heavy casualties on the encircled forces if we cannot capture them in large numbers. Only through the cumulative effect of many such battles of annihilation can we change the relative position as between the enemy and ourselves, thoroughly smash his strategic encirclement -- that is, his scheme of exterior-line operations -- and finally, in co-ordination with international forces and the revolutionary struggles of the Japanese people, surround the Japanese imperialists and deal them the coup de grace. These results are to be achieved mainly through regular warfare, with guerrilla warfare making a secondary contribution. What is common to both, however, is the accumulation of many minor victories to make a major victory. Herein lies the great strategic role of guerrilla warfare in the War of Resistance.

Now let us discuss initiative, flexibility and planning in guerrilla warfare.

What is initiative in guerrilla warfare?

In any war, the opponents contend for the initiative, whether on a battlefield, in a battle area, in a war zone or in the whole war, for the initiative means freedom of action for an army. Any army which, losing the initiative, is forced into a passive position and ceases to have freedom of action, faces the danger of defeat or extermination. Naturally, gaining the initiative is harder in strategic defensive and interior-line operations and easier in offensive exterior-line operations. However, Japanese imperialism has two basic weaknesses, namely, its shortage of troops and the fact that it is fighting on foreign soil. Moreover, its underestimation of China's strength and the internal contradictions among the Japanese militarists have given rise to many mistakes in command, such as piecemeal reinforcement, lack of strategic co-ordination, occasional absence of a main direction for attack, failure to grasp opportunities in some operations and failure to wipe out encircled forces, all of which may be considered the third weakness of Japanese imperialism. Thus, despite the advantage of being on the offensive and operating on exterior lines, the Japanese militarists are gradually losing the initiative, because of their shortage of troops (their small territory, small population, inadequate resources, feudalistic imperialism, etc.), because of the fact that they are fighting on foreign soil (their war is imperialist and barbarous) and because of their stupidities in command. Japan is neither willing nor able to conclude the war at present, nor has her strategic offensive yet come to an end, but, as the general trend shows, her offensive is confined within certain limits, which is the inevitable consequence of her three weaknesses; she cannot go on indefinitely till she swallows the whole of China. Already there are signs that Japan will one day find herself in an utterly passive position. China, on the other hand, was in a rather passive position at the beginning of the war, but, having gained experience, she is now turning to the new policy of mobile warfare, the policy of taking the offensive, seeking quick decisions and operating on exterior lines in campaigns and battles, which, together with the policy of developing widespread guerrilla warfare, is helping China to build up a position of initiative day by day.

The question of the initiative is even more vital in guerrilla warfare. For most guerrilla units operate in very difficult circumstances, fighting without a rear, with their own weak forces facing the enemy's strong forces, lacking experience (when the units are newly organized), being separated, etc. Nevertheless, it is possible to build up the initiative in guerrilla warfare, the essential condition being to seize on the enemy's three weaknesses. Taking advantage of the enemy's shortage of troops (from the viewpoint of the war as a whole), the guerrilla units can boldly use vast areas as their fields of operation; taking advantage of the fact that the enemy is an alien invader and is pursuing a most barbarous policy, the guerrilla units can boldly enlist the support of millions upon millions of people; and taking advantage of the stupidities in the enemy's command, the guerrilla units can give full scope to their resourcefulness. While the regular army must seize on all these weaknesses of the enemy and turn them to good account in order to defeat him, it is even more important for the guerrilla units to do so. As for the guerrilla units' own weaknesses, they can be gradually reduced in the course of the struggle. Moreover, these weaknesses sometimes constitute the very condition for gaining the initiative. For example, it is precisely because the guerrilla units are small that they can mysteriously appear and disappear in their operations behind enemy lines, without the enemy's being able to do anything about them, and thus enjoy a freedom of action such as massive regular armies never can.

When the enemy is making a converging attack from several directions, a guerrilla unit can exercise initiative only with difficulty and can lose it all too easily. In such a case, if its appraisals and dispositions are wrong, it is liable to get into a passive position and consequently fail to smash the converging enemy attack. This may occur even when the enemy is on the defensive and we are on the offensive. For the initiative results from making a correct appraisal of the situation (both our own and that of the enemy) and from making the correct military and political dispositions. A pessimistic appraisal out of accord with the objective conditions and the passive dispositions ensuing from it will undoubtedly result in the loss of the initiative and throw one into a passive position. On the other hand, an over-optimistic appraisal out of accord with the objective conditions and the risky (unjustifiably risky) dispositions ensuing from it will also result in the loss of the initiative and eventually land one in a position similar to that of the pessimists. The initiative is not an innate attribute of genius, but is something an intelligent leader attains through open-minded study and correct appraisal of the objective conditions and through correct military and political dispositions. It follows that the initiative is not ready-made but is something that requires conscious effort.

When forced into a passive position through some incorrect appraisal and disposition or through overwhelming pressure, a guerrilla unit must strive to extricate itself. How this can be done depends on the circumstances. In many cases it is necessary to "move away". The ability to move is the distinctive feature of a guerrilla unit. To move away is the principal method for getting out of a passive position and regaining the initiative. But it is not the sole method. The moment when the enemy is most energetic and we are in the greatest difficulties is often the very moment when things begin to turn against him and in our favor. Frequently a favorable situation recurs and the initiative is regained as a result of "holding out a little longer".

Next, let us deal with flexibility.

Flexibility is a concrete expression of the initiative. The flexible employment of forces is more essential in guerrilla warfare than in regular warfare.

A guerrilla commander must understand that the flexible employment of his forces is the most important means of changing the situation as between the enemy and ourselves and of gaining the initiative. The nature of guerrilla warfare is such that guerrilla forces must be employed flexibly in accordance with the task in hand and with such circumstances as the state of the enemy, the terrain and the local population, and the chief ways of employing the forces are dispersal, concentration and shifting of position. In employing his forces, a guerrilla commander is like a fisherman casting his net, which he should be able to spread wide as well as draw in tight. When casting his net, the fisherman has to ascertain the depth of the water, the speed of the current and the presence or absence of obstructions; similarly, when dispersing his units, a guerrilla commander must take care not to incur losses through ignorance of the situation or through miscalculated action. Just as the fisherman must keep a grip on the cord in order to draw his net in tight, so the guerrilla commander must maintain liaison and communication with all his forces and keep enough of his main forces at hand. Just as a frequent change of position is necessary in fishing, so a frequent shift of position is necessary for a guerrilla unit. Dispersal, concentration and shifting of position are the three ways of flexibly employing forces in guerrilla warfare. Generally speaking, the dispersal of guerrilla units, or "breaking up the whole into parts", is employed chiefly: (1) when we want to threaten the enemy with a wide frontal attack because he is on the defensive, and there is temporarily no chance to mass our forces for action; (2) when we want to harass and disrupt the enemy throughout an area where his forces are weak; (3) when we are unable to break through the enemy's encirclement and try to slip away by making ourselves less conspicuous; (4) when we are restricted by terrain or supplies; or (5) when we are carrying on mass work over a wide area. But whatever the circumstances, when dispersing for action we should pay attention to the following: 1) we should never make an absolutely even dispersal of forces, but should keep a fairly large part in an area convenient for maneuver, so that any possible exigency can be met and there is a centre of gravity for the task being carried out in dispersion; and (2) we should assign to the dispersed units clearly defined tasks, fields of operation, time limits for actions, places for reassembly and ways and means of liaison.

Concentration of forces, or "assembling the parts into a whole", is the method usually applied to destroy an enemy when he is on the offensive and sometimes to destroy some of his stationary forces when he is on the defensive. Concentration of forces does not mean absolute concentration, but the massing of the main forces for use in one important direction while retaining or dispatching part of the forces for use in other directions to contain, harass or disrupt the enemy, or to carry on mass work.

Although the flexible dispersal or concentration of forces according to circumstances is the principal method in guerrilla warfare, we must also know how to shift (or transfer) our forces flexibly. When the enemy feels seriously threatened by guerrillas, he will send troops to attack or suppress them. Hence the guerrilla units will have to take stock of the situation. If advisable, they should fight where they are; if not, they should lose no time in shifting elsewhere. Sometimes, in order to crush the enemy units one by one, guerrilla units which have destroyed an enemy force in one place may immediately shift to another so as to wipe out a second enemy force; sometimes, finding it inadvisable to fight in one place, they may have to disengage quickly and fight the enemy elsewhere. If the enemy's forces in a certain place present a particularly serious threat, the guerrilla units should not linger, but should move off with lightning speed. In general, shifts of position should be made with secrecy and speed. In order to mislead, decoy and confuse the enemy, they should constantly use stratagems, such as making a feint to the east but attacking in the west, appearing now in the south and now in the north, hit-and-run attacks, and night actions.

Flexibility in dispersal, concentration and shifts of position is a concrete expression of the initiative in guerrilla warfare, whereas rigidness and inertia inevitably lead to passivity and cause unnecessary losses. But a commander proves himself wise not just by recognition of the importance of employing his forces flexibly but by skill in dispersing, concentrating or shifting them in good time according to the specific circumstances. This wisdom in sensing changes and choosing the right moment to act is not easily acquired; it can be gained only by those who study with a receptive mind and investigate and ponder diligently. Prudent consideration of the circumstances is essential to prevent flexibility from turning into impulsive action.

Lastly, we come to planning.

Without planning, victories in guerrilla warfare are impossible. Any idea that guerrilla warfare can be conducted in haphazard fashion indicates either a flippant attitude or ignorance of guerrilla warfare. The operations in a guerrilla zone as a whole, or those of a guerrilla unit or formation, must be preceded by as thorough planning as possible, by preparation in advance for every action. Grasping the situation, setting the tasks, disposing the forces, giving military and political training, securing supplies, putting the equipment in good order, making proper use of the people's help, etc. -- all these are part of the work of the guerrilla commanders, which they must carefully consider and conscientiously perform and check up on. There can be no initiative, no flexibility, and no offensive unless they do so. True, guerrilla conditions do not allow as high a degree of planning as do those of regular warfare, and it would be a mistake to attempt very thorough planning in guerrilla warfare. But it is necessary to plan as thoroughly as the objective conditions permit, for it should be understood that fighting the enemy is no joke.

The above points serve to explain the first of the strategic principles of guerrilla warfare, the principle of using initiative, flexibility and planning in conducting offensives within the defensive, battles of quick decision within protracted war, and exterior-line operations within interior-line operations. It is the key problem in the strategy of guerrilla warfare. The solution of this problem provides the major guarantee of victory in guerrilla warfare so far as military command is concerned.

Although a variety of matters have been dealt with here, they all revolve around the offensive in campaigns and battles. The initiative can be decisively grasped only after victory in an offensive. Every offensive operation must be organized on our initiative and not launched under compulsion. Flexibility in the employment of forces revolves around the effort to take the offensive, and planning likewise is necessary chiefly in order to ensure success in offensive operations. Measures of tactical defense are meaningless if they are divorced from their role of giving either direct or indirect support to an offensive. Quick decision refers to the tempo of an offensive, and exterior lines refer to its scope. The offensive is the only means of destroying the enemy and is also the principal means of self-preservation, while pure defense and retreat can play only a temporary and partial role in self-preservation and are quite useless for destroying the enemy.

The principle stated above is basically the same for both regular and guerrilla war; it differs to some degree only in its form of expression. But in guerrilla war it is both important and necessary to note this difference. It is precisely this difference in form which distinguishes the operational methods of guerrilla war from those of regular war. If we confuse the two different forms in which the principle is expressed, victory in guerrilla war will be impossible.

# Chapter 5

# Co-ordination with Regular Warfare

The second problem of strategy in guerrilla warfare is its co-ordination with regular warfare. It is a matter of clarifying the relation between guerrilla and regular warfare on the operational level, in the light of the nature of actual guerrilla operations. An understanding of this relation is very important for effectiveness in defeating the enemy.

There are three kinds of co-ordination between guerrilla and regular warfare, co-ordination in strategy, in campaigns and in battles.

Taken as a whole, guerrilla warfare behind the enemy lines, which cripples the enemy, pins him down, disrupts his supply lines and inspires the regular forces and the people throughout the country, is co-ordinated with regular warfare in strategy. Take the case of the guerrilla warfare in the three northeastern provinces. Of course, the question of co-ordination did not arise before the nation-wide War of Resistance, but since the war began the significance of such co-ordination has become obvious. Every enemy soldier the guerrillas kill there, every bullet they make the enemy expend, every enemy soldier they stop from advancing south of the Great Wall, can be reckoned a contribution to the total strength of the resistance. It is, moreover, clear that they are having a demoralizing effect on the whole enemy army and all Japan and a heartening effect on our whole army and people. Still clearer is the role in strategic co-ordination played by the guerrilla warfare along the Peiping-Suiyuan, Peiping-Hankow, Tientsin-Pukow, Tatung-Puchow, Chengting-Taiyuan and Shanghai-Hangchow

Railways. Not only are the guerrilla units performing the function of co-ordination with the regular forces in our present strategic defensive, when the enemy is on the strategic offensive; not only will they co-ordinate with the regular forces in disrupting the enemy's hold on the occupied territory, after he concludes his strategic offensive and switches to the safeguarding of his gains; they will also co-ordinate with the regular forces in driving out the enemy forces and recovering all the lost territories, when the regular forces launch the strategic counter-offensive. The great role of guerrilla warfare in strategic co-ordination must not be overlooked. The commanders both of the guerrilla units and of the regular forces must clearly understand this role.

In addition, guerrilla warfare performs the function of co-ordination with regular warfare in campaigns. For instance, in the campaign at Hsinkou, north of Taiyuan, the guerrillas played a remarkable role in co-ordination both north and south of Yenmenkuan by wrecking the Tatung-Puchow Railway and the motor roads running through Pinghsingkuan and Yangfangkou. Or take another instance. After the enemy occupied Fenglingtu, guerrilla warfare, which was already widespread throughout Shansi Province and was conducted mainly by the regular forces, played an even greater role through co-ordination with the defensive campaigns west of the Yellow River in Shensi Province and south of the Yellow River in Honan Province. Again, when the enemy attacked southern Shantung, the guerrilla warfare in the five provinces of northern China contributed a great deal through co-ordination with the campaigns of our army. In performing a task of this sort, the leaders of each guerrilla base behind the enemy lines, or the commanders of a guerrilla formation temporarily dispatched there, must dispose their forces well and, by adopting different tactics suited to the time and place, move energetically against the enemy's most vital and vulnerable spots in order to cripple him, pin him down, disrupt his supply lines, inspire our armies campaigning on the interior lines, and so fulfill their duty of co-ordinating with the campaign. If each guerrilla zone or unit goes it alone without giving any attention to co-ordinating with the campaigns of the regular forces, its role in strategic co-ordination will lose a great deal of its significance, although it will still play some such role in the general strategy. All guerrilla commanders should give this point serious attention. To achieve co-ordination in campaigns, it is absolutely necessary for all larger guerrilla units and guerrilla formations to have radio equipment.

Finally, co-ordination with the regular forces in battles, in actual fighting on the battlefield, is the task of all guerrilla units in the vicinity of an interior-line battlefield. Of course, this applies only to guerrilla units operating close to the regular forces or to units of regulars dispatched on temporary guerrilla missions. In such cases, a guerrilla unit has to perform whatever task it is assigned by the commander of the regular forces, which is usually to pin down some of the enemy's forces, disrupt his supply lines, conduct reconnaissance, or act as guides for the regular forces. Even without such an assignment, the guerrilla unit should carry out these tasks on its own initiative. To sit by idly, neither moving nor fighting, or to move about without fighting, would be an intolerable attitude for a guerrilla unit.

# Chapter 6

# The Establishment of the Base Area

The third problem of strategy in anti-Japanese guerrilla warfare is the establishment of base areas, which is important and essential because of the protracted nature and ruthlessness of the war. The recovery of our lost territories will have to await the nation-wide strategic counter-offensive; by then the enemy's front will have extended deep into central China and cut it in two from north to south, and a part or even a greater part of our territory will have fallen into the hands of the enemy and become his rear. We shall have to extend guerrilla warfare all over this vast enemy-occupied area, make a front out of the enemy's rear, and force him to fight ceaselessly throughout the territory he occupies. Until such time as our strategic counter-offensive is launched and so long as our lost territories are not recovered, it will be necessary to persist in guerrilla warfare in the enemy's rear, certainly for a fairly long time, though one cannot say definitely for how long. This is why the war will be a protracted one. And in order to safeguard his gains in the occupied areas, the enemy is bound to step up his anti-guerrilla measures and, especially after the halting of his strategic offensive, to embark on relentless suppression of the guerrillas. With ruthlessness thus added to protractedness, it will be impossible to sustain guerrilla warfare behind the enemy lines without base areas.

What, then, are these base areas? They are the strategic bases on which the guerrilla forces rely in performing their strategic tasks and achieving the object of preserving and expanding themselves and destroying and driving out the enemy. Without such strategic bases, there will be nothing to depend on in carrying out any of our strategic tasks or achieving the aim of the war. It is a characteristic of guerrilla warfare behind the enemy lines that it is fought without a rear, for the guerrilla forces are severed from the country's general rear. But guerrilla warfare could not last long or grow without base areas. The base areas, indeed, are its rear.

History knows many peasant wars of the "roving rebel" type, but none of them ever succeeded. In the present age of advanced communications and technology, it would be all the more groundless to imagine that one can win victory by fighting in the manner of roving rebels. However, this roving-rebel idea still exists among impoverished peasants, and in the minds of guerrilla commanders it becomes the view that base areas are neither necessary nor important. Therefore, ridding the minds of guerrilla commanders of this idea is a prerequisite for deciding on a policy of establishing base areas. The question of whether or not to have base areas and of whether or not to regard them as important, in other words, the conflict between the idea of establishing base areas and that of fighting like roving rebels, arises in all guerrilla warfare, and, to a certain extent, our anti-Japanese guerrilla warfare is no exception. Therefore the struggle against the roving-rebel ideology is an inevitable process. Only when this ideology is thoroughly overcome and the policy of establishing base areas is initiated and applied will there be conditions favorable for the maintenance of guerrilla warfare over a long period.

Now that the necessity and importance of base areas have been made clear, let us pass on to the following problems which must be understood and solved when it comes to establishing the base areas. These problems are the types of base areas, the guerrilla zones and the base areas, the conditions for establishing base areas, their consolidation and expansion, and the forms in which we and the enemy encircle one another.

## 1. THE TYPES OF BASE AREAS

Base areas in anti-Japanese guerrilla warfare are mainly of three types, those in the mountains, those on the plains and those in the river-lake-estuary regions.

The advantage of setting up base areas in mountainous regions is obvious, and those which have been, are being or will be established in the Changpai,[1] Wutai,[2] Taihang,[3] Taishan,[4] Yenshan [5] and Maoshan [6] Mountains all belong to this type. They are all places where anti-Japanese guerrilla warfare can be maintained for the longest time and are important strongholds for the War of Resistance. We must develop guerrilla warfare and set up base areas in all the mountainous regions behind the enemy lines.

Of course, the plains are less suitable than the mountains, but it is by no means impossible to develop guerrilla warfare or establish any base areas there. Indeed, the widespread guerrilla warfare in the plains of Hopei and of northern and northwestern Shantung proves that it is possible to develop guerrilla warfare in the plains. While there is as yet no evidence on the possibility of setting up base areas there and maintaining them for long, it has been proved that the setting up of temporary base areas is possible, and it should be possible to set up base areas for small units or for seasonal use. On the one hand, the enemy does not have enough troops at his disposal and is pursuing a policy of unparalleled brutality, and on the other hand, China has a vast territory and vast numbers of people who are resisting Japan; the objective conditions for spreading guerrilla warfare and setting up temporary base areas in the plains are therefore fulfilled. Given competent military command, it should of course be possible to establish bases for small guerrilla units there, bases which are long-term but not fixed.[7] Broadly speaking, when the strategic offensive of the enemy is brought to a halt and he enters the stage of safeguarding his occupied areas, he will undoubtedly launch savage attacks on all the guerrilla base areas, and those in the plains will naturally be the first to bear the brunt. The large guerrilla formations operating on the plains will be unable to keep on fighting there for long and will gradually have to move up into the mountains as the circumstances require, as for instance, from the Hopei Plain to the Wutai and Taihang Mountains, or from the Shantung Plain to Taishan Mountain and the Shantung Peninsula in the east. But in the circumstances of our national war it is not impossible for numerous small guerrilla units to keep going in various counties over the vast plains and adopt a fluid way of fighting, i.e., by shifting their bases from place to place. It is definitely possible to conduct seasonal guerrilla warfare by taking advantage of the "green curtain" of tall crops in summer and of the frozen rivers in winter. As the enemy has no strength to spare now and will never be able to attend to everything even when he has the strength to spare, it is absolutely necessary for us to decide on the policy, for the present, of spreading guerrilla warfare far and wide and setting up temporary base areas in the plains and, for the future, of preparing to keep up guerrilla warfare by small units, if only seasonally, and of creating base areas which are not fixed.

Objectively speaking, the possibilities of developing guerrilla warfare and establishing base areas are greater in the river-lake-estuary regions than in the plains, though less than in the mountains. The dramatic battles fought by "pirates" and "water-bandits", of which our history is full, and the guerrilla warfare round the Hunghu Lake kept up for several years in the Red Army period, both testify to the possibility of developing guerrilla warfare and of establishing base areas in the river-lake-estuary regions. So far, however, the political parties and the masses who are resisting Japan have given this possibility little attention. Though the subjective conditions are as yet lacking, we should undoubtedly turn our attention to this possibility and start working on it. As one aspect in the development of our nation-wide guerrilla warfare, we should effectively organize guerrilla warfare in the Hungtse Lake region north of the Yangtse River, in the Taihu Lake region south of the Yangtse, and in all river-lake-estuary regions in the enemy-occupied areas along the rivers and on the seacoast, and we should create permanent base areas in and near such places. By overlooking this aspect we are virtually providing the enemy with water transport facilities; this is a gap in our strategic plan for the War of Resistance which must be filled in good time.

## 2. GUERRILLA ZONES AND BASE AREAS

In guerrilla warfare behind the enemy lines, there is a difference between guerrilla zones and base areas. Areas which are surrounded by the enemy but whose central parts are not occupied or have been recovered, like some counties in the Wutai mountain region (i.e., the Shansi-Chahar-Hopei border area) and also some places in the Taihang and Taishan mountain regions, are ready-made bases for the convenient use of guerrilla units in developing guerrilla warfare. But elsewhere in these areas the situation is different, as for instance in the eastern and northern sections of the Wutai mountain region, which include parts of western Hopei and southern Chahar, and in many places east of Paoting and west of Tsangchow. When guerrilla warfare began, the guerrillas could not completely occupy these places but could only make frequent raids; they are areas which are held by the guerrillas when they are there and by the puppet regime when they are gone, and are therefore not yet guerrilla bases but only what may be called guerrilla zones. Such guerrilla zones will be transformed into base areas when they have gone through the necessary processes of guerrilla warfare, that is, when large numbers of enemy troops have been annihilated or defeated there, the puppet regime has been destroyed, the masses have been roused to activity, anti-Japanese mass organizations have been formed, people's local armed forces have been developed, and anti-Japanese political power has been established. By the expansion of our base areas we mean the addition of areas such as these to the bases already established.

In some places, for example, eastern Hopei, the whole area of guerrilla operations has been a guerrilla zone from the very beginning. The puppet regime is of long standing there, and from the beginning the whole area of operations has been a guerrilla zone both for the people's armed forces that have grown out of local uprisings and for the guerrilla detachments dispatched from the Wutai Mountains. At the outset of their activities, all they could do was to choose some fairly good spots there as temporary rear or base areas. Such places will not be transformed from guerrilla zones into relatively stable base areas until the enemy forces are destroyed and the work of arousing the people is in full swing.

Thus the transformation of a guerrilla zone into a base area is an arduous creative process, and its accomplishment depends on the extent to which the enemy is destroyed and the masses are aroused.

Many regions will remain guerrilla zones for a long time. In these regions the enemy will not be able to set up stable puppet regimes, however much he tries to maintain control, while we, on our part, will not be able to achieve the aim of establishing anti-Japanese political power, however much we develop guerrilla warfare. Examples of this kind are to be found in the enemy-occupied regions along the railway lines, in the neighborhood of big cities and in certain areas in the plains.

As for the big cities, the railway stops and the areas in the plains which are strongly garrisoned by the enemy, guerrilla warfare can only extend to the fringes and not right into these places which have relatively stable puppet regimes. This is another kind of situation.

Mistakes in our leadership or strong enemy pressure may cause a reversal of the state of affairs described above, i.e., a guerrilla base may turn into a guerrilla zone, and a guerrilla zone may turn into an area under relatively stable enemy occupation. Such changes are possible, and they deserve special vigilance on the part of guerrilla commanders.

Therefore, as a result of guerrilla warfare and the struggle between us and the enemy, the entire enemy-occupied territory will fall into the following three categories: first, anti-Japanese bases held by our guerrilla units and our organs of political power; second, areas held by Japanese imperialism and its puppet regimes; and third, intermediate zones contested by both sides, namely, guerrilla zones. Guerrilla commanders have the duty to expand the first and third categories to the maximum and to reduce the second category to the minimum. This is the strategic task of guerrilla warfare.

## 3. CONDITIONS FOR ESTABLISHING BASE AREAS

The fundamental conditions for establishing a base area are that there should be anti-Japanese armed forces, that these armed forces should be employed to inflict defeats on the enemy and that they should arouse the people to action. Thus the establishment of a base area is first and foremost a matter of building an armed force. Leaders in guerrilla war must devote their energy to building one or more guerrilla units, and must gradually develop them in the course of struggle into guerrilla formations or even into units and formations of regular troops. The building up of an armed force is the key to establishing a base area; if there is no armed force or if the armed force is weak, nothing can be done. This constitutes the first condition.

The second indispensable condition for establishing a base area is that the armed forces should be used in co-ordination with the people to defeat the enemy. All places under enemy control are enemy, and not guerrilla, base areas, and obviously cannot be transformed into guerrilla base areas unless the enemy is defeated. Unless we repulse the enemy's attacks and defeat him, even places held by the guerrillas will come under enemy control, and then it will be impossible to establish base areas.

The third indispensable condition for establishing a base area is the use of all our strength, including our armed forces, to arouse the masses for struggle against Japan. In the course of this struggle we must arm the people, i.e., organize self-defense corps and guerrilla units. In the course of this struggle, we must form mass organizations, we must organize the workers, peasants, youth, women, children, merchants and professional people -- according to the degree of their political consciousness and fighting enthusiasm -- into the various mass organizations necessary for the struggle against Japanese aggression, and we must gradually expand them. Without organization, the people cannot give effect to their anti-Japanese strength. In the course of this struggle, we must weed out the open and the hidden traitors a task which can be accomplished only by relying on the strength of the people. In this struggle, it is particularly important to arouse the people to establish, or to consolidate, their local organs of anti-Japanese political power. Where the original Chinese organs of political power have not been destroyed by the enemy, we must re-organize and strengthen them with the support of the broad masses, and where they have been destroyed by the enemy, we should rebuild them by the efforts of the masses. They are organs of political power for carrying out the policy of the Anti-Japanese National United Front and should unite all the forces of the people to fight against our sole enemy, Japanese imperialism, and its jackals, the traitors and reactionaries.

A base area for guerrilla war can be truly established only with the gradual fulfillment of the three basic conditions, i.e., only after the anti-Japanese armed forces are built up, the enemy has suffered defeats and the people are aroused.

Mention must also be made of geographical and economic conditions. As for the former, we have already discussed three different categories in the earlier section on the types of base areas, and here we need only mention one major requirement, namely, that the area must be extensive. In places surrounded by the enemy on all sides, or on three sides, the mountainous regions naturally offer the best conditions for setting up base areas which can hold out for a long time, but the main thing is that there must be enough room for the guerrillas to maneuver, namely, the areas have to be extensive. Given an extensive area, guerrilla warfare can be developed and sustained even in the plains, not to mention the river-lake-estuary regions. By and large, the vastness of China's territory and the enemy's shortage of troops provide guerrilla warfare in China with this condition. This is an important, even a primary condition, as far as the possibility of waging guerrilla warfare is concerned, and small countries like Belgium which lack this condition have few or no such possibilities.[8] In China, this condition is not something which has to be striven for, nor does it present a problem; it is there physically, waiting only to be exploited.

So far as their physical setting is concerned, the economic conditions resemble the geographical conditions. For now we are discussing the establishment of base areas not in a desert, where no enemy is to be found, but behind the enemy lines; every place the enemy can penetrate already has its Chinese inhabitants and an economic basis for subsistence, so that the question of choice of economic conditions in establishing base areas simply does not arise. Irrespective of the economic conditions, we should do our utmost to develop guerrilla warfare and set up permanent or temporary base areas in all places where Chinese inhabitants and enemy forces are to be found. In a political sense, however, the economic conditions do present a problem, a problem of economic policy which is of immense importance to the establishment of base areas. The economic policy of the guerrilla base areas must follow the principles of the Anti-Japanese National United Front by equitably distributing the financial burden and protecting commerce. Neither the local organs of political power nor the guerrilla units must violate these principles, or otherwise the establishment of base areas and the maintenance of guerrilla warfare would be adversely affected. The equitable distribution of the financial burden means that "those with money should contribute money", while the peasants should supply the guerrilla units with grain within certain limits. The protection of commerce means that the guerrilla units should be highly disciplined and that the confiscation of shops, except those owned by proved traitors, should be strictly prohibited. This is no easy matter, but the policy is set and must be put into effect.

## 4. THE CONSOLIDATION AND EXPANSION OF BASE AREAS

In order to confine the enemy invaders to a few strongholds, that is, to the big cities and along the main communication lines, the guerrillas must do all they can to extend guerrilla warfare from their base areas as widely as possible and hem in all the enemy's strongholds, thus threatening his existence and shaking his morale while expanding the base areas. This is essential. In this context, we must oppose conservatism in guerrilla warfare. Whether originating in the desire for an easy life or in overestimation of the enemy's strength, conservatism can only bring losses in the War of Resistance and is harmful to guerrilla warfare and to the base areas themselves. At the same time, we must not forget the consolidation of the base areas, the chief task being to arouse and organize the masses and to train guerrilla units and local armed forces. Such consolidation is needed for maintaining protracted warfare and also for expansion, and in its absence energetic expansion is impossible. If we attend only to expansion and forget about consolidation in our guerrilla warfare, we shall be unable to withstand the enemy's attacks, and consequently not only forfeit the possibility of expansion but also endanger the very existence of the base areas. The correct principle is expansion with consolidation, which is a good method and allows us to take the offensive or the defensive as we choose. Given a protracted war, the problem of consolidating and expanding base areas constantly arises for every guerrilla unit. The concrete solution depends, of course, on the circumstances. At one time, the emphasis may be on expansion, i.e., on expanding the guerrilla zones and increasing the number of guerrillas. At another, the emphasis may be on consolidation, i.e., on organizing the masses and training the troops. As expansion and consolidation differ in nature, and as the military dispositions and other tasks will differ accordingly, an effective solution of the problem is possible only if we alternate the emphasis according to time and circumstances.

## 5. FORMS IN WHICH WE AND THE ENEMY ENCIRCLE ONE ANOTHER

Taking the War of Resistance as a whole, there is no doubt that we are strategically encircled by the enemy, because he is on the strategic offensive and is operating on exterior lines while we are on the strategic defensive and are operating on interior lines. This is the first form of enemy encirclement. We on our part encircle each of the enemy columns advancing on us along separate routes, because we apply the policy of the offensive and of exterior-line operations in campaigns and battles by using numerically preponderant forces against these enemy columns advancing on us from exterior lines. This is the first form of our encirclement of the enemy. Next, if we consider the guerrilla base areas in the enemy's rear, each area taken singly is surrounded by the enemy on all sides, like the Wutai mountain region, or on three sides, like the northwestern Shansi area. This is the second form of enemy encirclement. However, if one considers all the guerrilla base areas together and in their relation to the battle fronts of the regular forces, one can see that we in turn surround a great many enemy forces. In Shansi Province, for instance, we have surrounded the Tatung-Puchow Railway on three sides (the east and west flanks and the southern end) and the city of Taiyuan on all sides; and there are many similar instances in Hopei and Shantung Provinces. This is the second form of our encirclement of the enemy. Thus there are two forms of encirclement by the enemy forces and two forms of encirclement by our own -- rather like a game of weichi.[9] Campaigns and battles fought by the two sides resemble the capturing of each other's pieces, and the establishment of strongholds by the enemy and of guerrilla base areas by us resembles moves to dominate spaces on the board. It is in the matter of "dominating the spaces" that the great strategic role of guerrilla base areas in the rear of the enemy is revealed.

We are raising this question in the War of Resistance in order that the nation's military authorities and the guerrilla commanders in all areas should place on the agenda the development of guerrilla warfare behind the enemy lines and the establishment of base areas wherever possible, and carry this out as a strategic task. If on the international plane we can create an anti-Japanese front in the Pacific region, with China as one strategic unit, and the Soviet Union and other countries which may join it as other strategic units, we shall then have one more form of encirclement against the enemy than he has against us and bring about exterior-line operations in the Pacific region by which to encircle and destroy fascist Japan.

To be sure, this is of little practical significance at present, but such a prospect is not impossible.

# Chapter 7

# The Strategic Defensive and the Strategic Offensive in Guerrilla War

The fourth problem of strategy in guerrilla war concerns the strategic defensive and the strategic offensive. This is the problem of how the policy of offensive warfare, which we mentioned in our discussion of the first problem, is to be carried out in practice, when we are on the defensive and when we are on the offensive in our guerrilla warfare against Japan.

Within the nation-wide strategic defensive or strategic offensive (to be more exact, the strategic counter-offensive), small-scale strategic defensives and offensives take place in and around each guerrilla base area. By strategic defensive we mean our strategic situation and policy when the enemy is on the offensive and we are on the defensive; by strategic offensive we mean our strategic situation and policy when the enemy is on the defensive and we are on the offensive.

## 1. THE STRATEGIC DEFENSIVE IN GUERRILLA WAR

After guerrilla warfare has broken out and grown to a considerable extent, the enemy will inevitably attack the guerrilla base areas, especially in the period when his strategic offensive against the country as a whole is brought to an end and he adopts the policy of safeguarding his occupied areas. It is essential to recognize the inevitability of such attacks, for otherwise the guerrilla commanders will be caught wholly unprepared, and in the face of heavy enemy attacks they will undoubtedly become alarmed and confused and their forces will be routed.

To wipe out the guerrillas and their base areas, the enemy frequently resorts to converging attacks. For instance, in each of the four or five "punitive expeditions" directed against the Wutai mountain region, the enemy made a planned advance in three, four or even six or seven columns simultaneously. The larger the scale of the guerrilla fighting, the more important the position of the base areas, and the greater the threat to the enemy's strategic centers and vital communication lines, the fiercer will be the enemy's attacks. Therefore, the fiercer the enemy's attacks on a guerrilla area, the greater the indication that the guerrilla warfare there is successful and is being effectively co-ordinated with the regular fighting.

When the enemy launches a converging attack in several columns, the guerrilla policy should be to smash it by counter-attack. It can be easily smashed if each advancing enemy column consists of only one unit, whether big or small, has no follow-up units and is unable to station troops along the route of advance, construct blockhouses or build motor roads. When the enemy launches a converging attack, he is on the offensive and operating on exterior lines, while we are on the defensive and operating on interior lines. As for our dispositions, we should use our secondary forces to pin down several enemy columns, while our main force should launch surprise attacks (chiefly in the form of ambushes) in a campaign or battle against a single enemy column, striking it when it is on the move. The enemy, though strong, will be weakened by repeated surprise attacks and will often withdraw when he is halfway; the guerrilla units can then make more surprise attacks during the pursuit and weaken him still further. The enemy generally occupies the county towns or other towns in our base areas before he stops his offensive or begins to withdraw, and we should encircle these towns, cutting off his grain supply and severing his communications, so that when he cannot hold out and begins to retreat, we can seize the opportunity to pursue and attack him. After smashing one column, we should shift our forces to smash another, and, by smashing them one by one, shatter the converging attack.

A big base area like the Wutai mountain region forms a military area, which is divided into four or five, or even more, military sub-areas, each with its own armed forces operating independently. By employing the tactics described above, these forces have often smashed the enemy's attacks simultaneously or successively.

In our plan of operations against a converging attack by the enemy, we generally place our main force on interior lines. But when we have the strength to spare, we should use our secondary forces (such as the county or the district guerrilla units, or even detachments of the main force) on exterior lines to disrupt the enemy's communications and pin down his reinforcements. Should the enemy stay put in our base area, we may reverse the tactics, namely, leave some of our forces in the base area to invest the enemy while employing the main force to attack the region whence he has come and to step up our activities there, in order to induce him to withdraw and attack our main force; this is the tactic of "relieving the state of Chao by besieging the state of Wei".[10]

In the course of operations against a converging attack, the local anti-Japanese self-defense corps and all the mass organizations should mobilize for action and in every way help our troops to fight the enemy. In fighting the enemy, it is important both to enforce local martial law and, as far as possible, to "strengthen our defense works and clear the fields". The purpose of the former is to suppress traitors and prevent the enemy from getting information, and of the latter to assist our own operations (by strengthening our defense works) and prevent the enemy from getting food (by clearing the fields). "Clearing the fields" means harvesting the crops as soon as they are ripe.

When the enemy retreats, he often burns down the houses in the cities and towns he has occupied and razes the villages along his route, with the purpose of destroying the guerrilla base areas; but in so doing he deprives himself of shelter and food in his next offensive, and the damage recoils upon his own head. This is a concrete illustration of what we mean by one and the same thing having two contradictory aspects.

A guerrilla commander should not think of abandoning his base area and shifting to another, unless it proves impossible, after repeated operations, to smash the enemy's heavy converging attacks. In these circumstances he must guard against pessimism. So long as the leaders do not blunder in matters of principle, it is generally possible to smash the converging attacks and hold on to the base areas in the mountainous regions. It is only in the plains that, when confronted by a heavy converging attack, the guerrilla commander should consider other measures in the light of the specific circumstances, namely, leaving many small units for scattered operations, while temporarily shifting large guerrilla formations to some mountainous region, so that they can return and resume their activities in the plains once the main forces of the enemy move away.

Generally speaking, the Japanese cannot adopt the principle of blockhouse warfare, which the Kuomintang employed in the days of the civil war, because their forces are inadequate in relation to China's vast territory. However, we should reckon with the possibility that they may use it to some extent against those guerrilla base areas which pose a particular threat to their vital positions, but even in such circumstances we should be prepared to keep up guerrilla warfare n those areas. Since we have had the experience of being able to maintain guerrilla warfare during the civil war, there is not the slightest doubt of our greater capacity to do so in a national war. Though, in point of relative military strength, the enemy can throw forces that are vastly superior in quantity as well as in quality against some of our base areas, there remain the insoluble national contradiction between us and the enemy and the unavoidable weaknesses of his command. Our victories are based on thorough work among the masses and flexible tactics in our operations.

## 2. THE STRATEGIC OFFENSIVE IN GUERRILLA WAR

After we have smashed an enemy offensive and before the enemy starts a new offensive, he is on the strategic defensive and we are on the strategic offensive.

At such times our operational policy is not to attack enemy forces which are entrenched in defensive positions and which we are not sure of defeating, but systematically to destroy or drive out the small enemy units and puppet forces in certain areas, which our guerrilla units are strong enough to deal with, and to expand our areas, arouse the masses for struggle against Japan, replenish and train our troops and organize new guerrilla units. If the enemy still remains on the defensive when these tasks are under way, we can expand our new areas still further and attack weakly garrisoned cities and communication lines and hold them for as long as circumstances permit. These are all tasks of the strategic offensive, and the purpose is to take advantage of the fact that the enemy is on the defensive so that we may effectively build up our own military and mass strength, effectively reduce the enemy's strength and prepare to smash the enemy methodically and vigorously when he mounts an offensive again.

It is essential to rest and train our troops, and the best time for doing so is when the enemy is on the defensive. It is not a question of shutting ourselves off from everything else for rest and training, but of finding time for rest and training while expanding our areas, mopping up small enemy units and arousing the people. This is usually also the time for tackling the difficult problem of getting food supplies, bedding, clothing, etc.

It is also the time for destroying the enemy's communication lines on a large scale, hampering his transport and giving direct support to the regular forces in their campaigns.

At such times the guerrilla base areas, guerrilla zones and guerrilla units are in high spirits, and the areas devastated by the enemy are gradually rehabilitated and revived. The people in the enemy-occupied territories are also delighted, and the fame of the guerrillas resounds everywhere. On the other hand, in the camp of the enemy and his running dogs, the traitors, panic and disintegration are mounting, while there is growing hatred of the guerrillas and their base areas and preparations to deal with them are intensified. During the strategic offensive, therefore, it is impermissible for the guerrilla commanders to become so elated as to underrate the enemy and forget to strengthen unity in their own ranks and to consolidate their base areas and their forces. At such times, they must skillfully watch the enemy's every move for signs of any new offensive against us, so that the moment it comes they can wind up their strategic offensive in good order, turn to the strategic defensive and thereby smash the enemy's offensive.

# Chapter 8

# Development of Guerrilla War into Mobile War

The fifth problem of strategy in guerrilla war against Japan is its development into mobile war, a development which is necessary and possible because the war is protracted and ruthless. If China could speedily defeat the Japanese invaders and recover her lost territories, and if the war were neither protracted nor ruthless, this would not be necessary. But as, on the contrary, the war is protracted and ruthless, guerrilla warfare cannot adapt itself to such a war except by developing into mobile warfare. Since the war is protracted and ruthless, it is possible for the guerrilla units to undergo the necessary steeling and gradually to transform themselves into regular forces, so that their mode of operations is gradually regularized and guerrilla warfare develops into mobile warfare. The necessity and possibility of this development must be clearly recognized by the guerrilla commanders if they are to persist in, and systematically carry out, the policy of turning guerrilla warfare into mobile warfare.

In many places, such as the Wutai mountain region, the present guerrilla warfare owes its growth to the strong detachments sent there by the regular forces. The operations there, though generally of a guerrilla character, have contained an element of mobile warfare from the very beginning. This element will gradually increase as the war goes on. Herein lies the advantage which makes possible the swift expansion of the present anti-Japanese guerrilla warfare and its rapid development to a higher level; thus the conditions for guerrilla warfare are far superior to what they were in the three northeastern provinces.

To transform guerrilla units waging guerrilla warfare into regular forces waging mobile warfare, two conditions are necessary -- an increase in numbers, and an improvement in quality. Apart from directly mobilizing the people to join the forces, increased numbers can be attained by amalgamating small units, while better quality depends on steeling the fighters and improving their weapons in the course of the war.

In amalgamating small units, we must, on the one hand, guard against localism, whereby attention is concentrated exclusively on local interests and centralization is impeded, and, on the other, guard against the purely military approach, whereby local interests are brushed aside.

Localism exists among the local guerrilla units and local governments, which are frequently preoccupied with local considerations to the neglect of the general interest, or which prefer to act each on its own because they are unaccustomed to acting in larger groups. The commanders of the main guerrilla units or of the guerrilla formations must take this into account and adopt the method of gradual amalgamation of part of the local units, allowing the localities to keep some of their forces and expand their guerrilla warfare; the commanders should draw these units into joint operations and then bring about their amalgamation without breaking up their original organization or reshuffling their cadres, so that the small groups may integrate smoothly into the larger group.

As against localism, the purely military approach represents the wrong viewpoint held in the main forces by those who are bent on expanding their own strength and who neglect to assist the local armed units. They do not realize that the development of guerrilla warfare into mobile warfare means not the abandonment of guerrilla warfare, but the gradual formation, in the midst of widespread guerrilla warfare, of a main force capable of conducting mobile warfare, a force around which there must still be numerous guerrilla units carrying on extensive guerrilla operations. These guerrilla units are powerful auxiliaries to the main force and serve as inexhaustible reserves for its continuous growth. Therefore, if a commander of a main force has made the mistake of neglecting the interests of the local population and the local government as a result of a purely military approach, he must correct it in order that the expansion of the main force and the multiplication of the local armed units may both receive due attention.

To raise the quality of the guerrilla units it is imperative to raise their political and organizational level and improve their equipment, military technique, tactics and discipline, so that they gradually pattern themselves on the regular forces and shed their guerrilla ways. Politically, it is imperative to get both the commanders and the fighters to realize the necessity of raising the guerrilla units to the level of the regular forces, to encourage them to strive towards this end, and to guarantee its attainment by means of political work. Organizationally, it is imperative gradually to fulfill all the requirements of a regular formation in the following respects -- military and political organs, staff and working methods, a regular supply system, a medical service, etc. In the matter of equipment, it is imperative to acquire: better and more varied weapons and increase the supply of the necessary communications equipment. In the matter of military technique and tactics, it is imperative to raise the guerrilla units to the level required of a regular formation. In the matter of discipline, it is imperative to raise the level so that uniform standards are observed, every order is executed without fail and all slackness is eliminated. To accomplish all these tasks requires a prolonged effort, and it cannot be done overnight; but that is the direction in which we must develop. Only thus can a main force be built up in each guerrilla base area and mobile warfare emerge for more effective attacks on the enemy. Where detachments or cadres have been sent in by the regular forces, the goal can be achieved more easily. Hence all the regular forces have the responsibility of helping the guerrilla units to develop into regular units.

# Chapter 9

# The Relationship of Command

The last problem of strategy in guerrilla war against Japan concerns the relationship of command. A correct solution of this problem is one of the prerequisites for the unhampered development of guerrilla warfare.

Since guerrilla units are a lower level of armed organization characterized by dispersed operations, the methods of command in guerrilla warfare do not allow as high a degree of centralization as in regular warfare. If any attempt is made to apply the methods of command in regular warfare to guerrilla warfare, its great flexibility will inevitably be restricted and its vitality sapped. A highly centralized command is in direct contradiction to the great flexibility of guerrilla warfare and must not and cannot be applied to it.

However, guerrilla warfare cannot be successfully developed without some centralized command. When extensive regular warfare and extensive guerrilla warfare are going on at the same time, their operations must be properly co-ordinated; hence the need for a command co-ordinating the two, i.e., for a unified strategic command by the national general staff and the war-zone commanders. In a guerrilla zone or guerrilla base area with many guerrilla units, there are usually one or more guerrilla formations (sometimes together with regular formations) which constitute the main force, a number of other guerrilla units, big and small, which represent the supplementary force, and many armed units composed of people not withdrawn from production; the enemy forces there usually form a unified complex to concert their operations against the guerrillas. Consequently, the problem arises of setting up a unified or centralized command in such guerrilla zones or base areas.

Hence, as opposed both to absolute centralization and to absolute decentralization, the principle of command in guerrilla war should be centralized strategic command and decentralized command in campaigns and battles.

Centralized strategic command includes the planning and direction of guerrilla warfare as a whole by the state, the co-ordination of guerrilla warfare with regular warfare in each war zone, and the unified direction of all the anti-Japanese armed forces in each guerrilla zone or base area. Here lack of harmony, unity and centralization is harmful, and every effort must be made to ensure all three. In general matters, that is, matters of strategy, the lower levels should report to the higher and follow their instructions so as to ensure concerted action. Centralization, however, stops at this point, and it would likewise be harmful to go beyond it and interfere with the lower levels in matters of detail like the specific dispositions for a campaign or battle. For such details must be settled in the light of specific conditions, which change from time to time and from place to place and are quite beyond the knowledge of the distant higher levels of command. This is what is meant by the principle of decentralized command in campaigns and battles. The same principle generally applies in regular operations, especially when communications are inadequate. In a word, it means guerrilla warfare waged independently and with the initiative in our hands within the framework of a unified strategy.

Where a guerrilla base area constitutes a military area divided into sub-areas, each comprising several counties, each of which is again divided into districts, the relationship between the various levels, from the headquarters of the military area and sub-areas down to the county and district governments, is one of consecutive subordination, and every armed force must, according to its nature, be under the direct command of one of these. On the principle that has been enunciated, in the relationship of command at these levels matters of general policy should be centralized in the higher levels, while actual operations should be carried out in the light of the specific circumstances by the lower levels, which should have the right of independent action. If a higher level has something to say about the actual operations undertaken at a lower level, it can and should advance its views as "instructions" but must not issue hard and fast "commands". The more extensive the area, the more complex the situation and the greater the distance between the higher and the lower levels, the more advisable it becomes to allow greater independence to the lower levels in their actual operations and thus give those operations a character conforming more closely to the local requirements, so that the lower levels and the local personnel may develop the ability to work independently, cope with complicated situations, and successfully expand guerrilla warfare. For an armed unit or bigger formation which is engaged in a concentrated operation, the principle to be applied is one of centralization in its internal relationship of command, since the situation is clear to the higher command but the moment this unit or formation breaks up for dispersed action, the principle of centralization in general matters and of decentralization in details should be applied, for then the specific situation cannot be clear to the higher command. Absence of centralization where it is needed means negligence by the higher levels or usurpation of authority by the lower levels, neither of which can be tolerated in the relationship between higher and lower levels, especially in the military sphere. If decentralization is not effected where it should be, that means monopolization of power by the higher levels and lack of initiative on the part of the lower levels, neither of which can be tolerated in the relationship between higher and lower levels, especially in the command of guerrilla war fare. The above principles constitute the only correct policy for solving the problem of the relationship of command.

# NOTES

[1] The Changpai mountain range is situated on the northeastern border of China. After the Japanese invasion on September 18, 1931, the region became a base area for the anti-Japanese guerrillas led by the Chinese Communist Party.

[2] The Wutai mountain range is situated on the borders between Shansi, Hopei and what was then Chahar Province. In October 1937 the Eighth Route Army led by the Chinese Communist Party started building the Shansi-Chahar-Hopei anti-Japanese base area with the Wutai mountain region as its centre.

[3] The Taihang mountain range is situated on the borders between Shansi, Hopei and Honan Provinces. In November 1937 the Eighth Route Army started building the southeastern Shansi anti-Japanese base area with the Taihang mountain region as its centre.

[4] The Taishan Mountain is one of the chief peaks of the Tai-Yi mountain range in central Shantung. In the winter of 1937 the guerrilla forces led by the Communist Party started building the central Shantung anti-Japanese base area with the Tai-Yi mountain region as its centre.

[5] The Yenshan mountain range is situated on the border of Hopei and what was then Jehol Province. In the summer of 1938 the Eighth Route Army started building the eastern Hopei anti-Japanese base area with the Yenshan mountain region as its centre.

[6] The Maoshan Mountains are in southern Kiangsu. In June 1938 the New Fourth Army led by the Communist Party

started building the southern Kiangsu anti-Japanese base area with the Maoshan mountain region as its centre.

[7] Experience gained in the War of Resistance proved that it was possible to establish long-term and, in many places, stable base areas in the plains. This was due to their vastness and big populations, the correctness of the Communist Party's policies, the extensive mobilization of the people and the enemy's shortage of troops. Comrade Mao Zedong affirmed this possibility more definitely in later directives.

[8] Ever since the end of World War II, the national and democratic revolutionary movement has been surging forward in Asia, Africa and Latin America. In many countries the people, led by their own revolutionary and progressive forces, have carried on sustained armed struggles to overthrow the dark rule of imperialism and reaction. This demonstrates that in the new historical circumstances -- when the socialist camp, the revolutionary forces of the people in the colonial countries and the forces of the people striving for democracy and progress in all countries are taking giant strides forward, when the world capitalist system is weakening still further, and when the colonial rule of imperialism is heading for disintegration -- the conditions under which the people of various countries conduct guerrilla warfare today need not be quite the same as those which were necessary in the days of the guerrilla warfare waged by the Chinese people against Japan. In other words, guerrilla war can be victoriously waged in a country which is not large in territory, as for instance, in Cuba, Algeria, Laos and southern Viet Nam.

[9] Weichi is an old Chinese game, in which the two players try to encircle each other's pieces on the board. When a player's pieces are encircled, they are counted as "dead" (captured). But

if there is a sufficient number of blank spaces among the encircled pieces, then the latter are still "alive" (not captured).

[10] In 353 B.C. the state of Wei laid siege to Hantan, capital of the state of Chao. The king of the state of Chi, an ally of Chao, ordered his generals Tien Chi and Sun Pin to aid Chao with their troops. Knowing that the crack forces of Wei had entered Chao and left their own territory weakly garrisoned, General Sun Pin attacked the state of Wei whose troops withdrew to defend their own country. Taking advantage of their exhaustion, the troops of Chi engaged and routed them at Kueiling (northeast of the present Hotse County in Shantung). The siege of Hantan, capital of Chao, was thus lifted. Since then Chinese strategists have referred to similar tactics as "relieving the state of Chao by besieging the state of Wei".

# COLLECTED WRITINGS
## OF
# CHAIRMAN MAO

## VOLUME 2

# GUERRILLA WARFARE

## PART 3

# ON PROTRACTED WAR

*Mao Zedong*

# *Preface*

This series of lectures was delivered by Mao Zedong from May 26 to June 3, 1938, at the Yenan Association for the Study of the War of Resistance against Japan.

*Mao Zedong*

## STATEMENT OF THE PROBLEM

1. It will soon be July 7, the first anniversary of the great War of Resistance against Japan. Rallying in unity, persevering in resistance and persevering in the united front, the forces of the whole nation have been valiantly fighting the enemy for almost a year. The people of the whole world are attentively following this war, which has no precedent in the history of the East, and which will go down as a great war in world history too. Every Chinese suffering from the disasters of the war and fighting for the survival of his nation daily yearns for victory. But what actually will be the course of the war? Can we win? Can we win quickly? Many people are talking about a protracted war, but why is it a protracted war? How to carry on a protracted war? Many people are talking about final victory, but why will final victory be ours? How shall we strive for final victory? Not everyone has found answers to these questions; in fact, to this day most people have not done so. Therefore the defeatist exponents of the theory of national subjugation have come forward to tell people that China will be subjugated, that final victory will not be China's. On the other hand, some impetuous friends have come forward to tell people that China will win very quickly without having to exert any great effort. But are these views correct? We have said all along they are not. However, most people have not yet grasped what we have been saying. This is partly because we did not do enough propaganda and explanatory work, and partly because the development of objective events had not yet fully and clearly revealed their inherent nature and their features to the people, who were thus not in a position to foresee the over-all trend and the outcome and hence to decide on a complete set of policies and tactics. Now things are better; the experience of ten months of war has been quite sufficient to explode the utterly baseless theory of national subjugation and to dissuade

our impetuous friends from their theory of quick victory. In these circumstances many people are asking for a comprehensive explanation. All the more so with regard to protracted war, not only because of the opposing theories of national subjugation and quick victory but also because of the shallow understanding of its nature. "Our four hundred million people have been making a concerted effort since the Lukouchiao Incident, and the final victory will belong to China." This formula has a wide currency. It is a correct formula but needs to be given more content. Our perseverance in the War of Resistance and in the united front has been possible because of many factors. Internally, they comprise all the political parties in the country from the Communist Party to the Kuomintang, all the people from the workers and peasants to the bourgeoisie, and all the armed forces from the regular forces to the guerrillas; internationally, they range from the land of socialism to justice-loving people in all countries; in the camp of the enemy, they range from those people in Japan who are against the war to those Japanese soldiers at the front who are against the war. In short, all these forces have contributed in varying degrees to our War of Resistance. Every man with a conscience should salute them. We Communists, together with all the other anti-Japanese political parties and the whole people, have no other course than to strive to unite all forces for the defeat of the diabolical Japanese aggressors. July 1 this year will be the 17th anniversary of the founding of the Communist Party of China. A serious study of protracted war is necessary in order to enable every Communist to play a better and greater part in the War of Resistance. Therefore my lectures will be devoted to such a study. I shall try- to speak on all the problems relevant to the protracted war, but I cannot possibly go into everything in one series of lectures.

2. All the experience of the ten months of war proves the error both of the theory of China's inevitable subjugation and

of the theory of China's quick victory. The former gives rise to the tendency to compromise and the latter to the tendency to underestimate the enemy. Both approaches to the problem are subjective and one-sided, or, in a word, unscientific.

3. Before the War of Resistance, there was a great deal of talk about national subjugation. Some said, "China is inferior in arms and is bound to lose in a war." Others said, "If China offers armed resistance, she is sure to become another Abyssinia." Since the beginning of the war, open talk of national subjugation has disappeared, but secret talk, and quite a lot of it too, still continues. For instance, from time to time an atmosphere of compromise arises and the advocates of compromise argue that "the continuance of the war spells subjugation". [1] In a letter from Hunan a student has written:

In the countryside everything seems difficult. Doing propaganda work on my own, I have to talk to people when and where I find them. The people I have talked to are by no means ignoramuses; they all have some understanding of what is going on and are very interested in what I have to say. But when I run into my own relatives, they always say: "China cannot win; she is doomed." They make one sick! Fortunately, they do not go around spreading their views, otherwise things would really be bad. The peasants would naturally put more stock in what they say.

Such exponents of the theory of China's inevitable subjugation form the social basis of the tendency to compromise. They are to be found everywhere in China, and therefore the problem of compromise is liable to crop up within the anti-Japanese front at any time and will probably remain with us right until the end of the war. Now that Hsuchow has fallen and Wuhan is in danger, it will not be unprofitable, I think, to knock the bottom out of the theory of national subjugation.

4. During these ten months of war all kinds of views which are indicative of impetuosity have also appeared. For instance, at the outset of the war many people were groundlessly optimistic, underestimating Japan and even believing that the Japanese could not get as far as Shansi. Some belittled the strategic role of guerrilla warfare in the War of Resistance and doubted the proposition, "With regard to the whole, mobile warfare is primary and guerrilla warfare supplementary; with regard to the parts, guerrilla warfare is primary and mobile warfare supplementary." They disagreed with the Eighth Route Army's strategy, "Guerrilla warfare is basic, but lose no chance for mobile warfare under favorable conditions", which they regarded as a "mechanical" approach. [2] During the battle of Shanghai some people said: "If we can fight for just three months, the international situation is bound to change, the Soviet Union is bound to send troops, and the war will be over." They pinned their hopes for the future of the War of Resistance chiefly on foreign aid. [3] After the Taierhchuang victory, [4] some people maintained that the Hsuchow campaign should be fought as a "quasi-decisive campaign" and that the policy of protracted war should be changed. They said such things as, "This campaign marks the last desperate struggle of the enemy," or, "If we win, the Japanese warlords will be demoralized and able only to await their Day of Judgment." [5] The victory at Pinghsingkuan turned some people's heads, and further victory at Taierhchuang has turned more people's heads. Doubts have arisen as to whether the enemy will attack Wuhan. Many people think "probably not", and many others "definitely not". Such doubts may affect all major issues. For instance, is our anti-Japanese strength already sufficient? Some people may answer affirmatively, for our present strength is already

sufficient to check the enemy's advance, so why increase it? Or, for instance, is the slogan "Consolidate and expand the Anti-Japanese National United Front" still correct? Some people may answer negatively, for the united front in its present state is already strong enough to repulse the enemy, so why consolidate and expand it? Or, for instance, should our efforts in diplomacy and international propaganda be intensified? Here again the answer may be in the negative. Or, for instance, should we proceed in earnest to reform the army system and the system of government, develop the mass movement, enforce education for national defense, suppress traitors and Trotskyites, develop war industries and improve the people's livelihood? Or, for instance, are the slogans calling for the defense of Wuhan, of Canton and of the Northwest and for the vigorous development of guerrilla warfare in the enemy's rear still correct? The answers might all be in the negative. There are even some people who, the moment a slightly favorable turn occurs in the war situation, are prepared to intensify the "friction" between the Kuomintang and the Communist Party, diverting attention from external to internal matters. This almost invariably occurs whenever a comparatively big battle is won or the enemy's advance comes to a temporary halt. All the above can be termed political and military short-sightedness. Such talk, however plausible, is actually specious and groundless. To sweep away such verbiage should help the victorious prosecution of the War of Resistance.

5. The question now is: Will China be subjugated? The answer is, No, she will not be subjugated, but will win final victory. Can China win quickly? The answer is, No, she cannot win quickly, and the War of Resistance will be a protracted war.

6.  As early as two years ago, we broadly indicated the main arguments on these questions. On July 16, 1936, five months before the Sian Incident and twelve months before the Lukouchiao Incident, in an interview with the American correspondent, Mr. Edgar Snow, I made a general estimate of the situation with regard to war between China and Japan and advanced various principles for winning victory. The following excerpts may serve as a reminder:

Question: Under what conditions do you think China can defeat and destroy the forces of Japan?

Answer: Three conditions are required: first, the establishment of an anti-Japanese united front in China; second, the formation of an international anti-Japanese united front; third, the rise of the revolutionary movement of the people in Japan and the Japanese colonies. From the standpoint of the Chinese people, the unity of the people of China is the most important of the three conditions.

Question: How long do you think such a war would last?

Answer: That depends on the strength of China's anti-Japanese united front and many other conditioning factors involving China and Japan. That is to say, apart from China's own strength, which is the main thing, international help to China and the help rendered by the revolution in Japan are also important. If China's anti-Japanese united front is greatly expanded and effectively organized horizontally and vertically, if the necessary help is given to China by those governments and peoples which recognize the Japanese imperialist menace to their own interests and if revolution comes quickly in Japan, the war will speedily be brought to an end and China will speedily win victory. If these conditions are not realized quickly, the war will be prolonged. But in the end, just the same, Japan will certainly be defeated and China will certainly be victorious. Only the sacrifices will be great and there will be a very painful period.

Question: What is your opinion of the probable course of development of such a war, politically and militarily?

Answer: Japan's continental policy is already fixed, and those who think they can halt the Japanese advance by making compromises with Japan at the expense of more Chinese territory and sovereign rights are indulging in mere fantasy. We definitely know that the lower Yangtse valley and our southern seaports are already included in the continental program of Japanese imperialism. Moreover, Japan wants to occupy the Philippines, Siam, Indo-China, the Malay Peninsula and the Dutch East Indies in order to cut off other countries from China and monopolize the southwestern Pacific. This is Japan's maritime policy. In such a period, China will undoubtedly be in an extremely difficult position. But the majority of the Chinese people believe that such difficulties can be overcome; only the rich in the big port cities are defeatists because they are afraid of losing their property. Many people think it would be impossible for China to continue the war, once her coastline is blockaded by Japan. This is nonsense. To refute them we need only cite the war history of the Red Army. In the present War of Resistance against Japan, China's position is much superior to that of the Red Army in the civil war. China is a vast country, and even if Japan should succeed in occupying a section of China with as many as 100 to 200 million people, we would still be far from defeated. We would still have ample strength to fight against Japan, while the Japanese would have to fight defensive battles in their rear throughout the war. The heterogeneity and uneven development of China's economy are rather advantageous in the war of resistance. For example, to sever Shanghai from the rest of China would definitely not be as disastrous to China as would be the severance of New York from the rest of the United States. Even if Japan blockades the Chinese coastline, it is impossible for her to blockade China's Northwest, Southwest and West. Thus, once more the central point of the problem is the unity of the entire Chinese people and the building up of a nation-wide anti-Japanese front. This is what we have long been advocating.

Question: If the war drags on for a long time and Japan is not completely defeated, would the Communist Party agree to the negotiation of a peace with Japan and recognize her rule in northeastern China?

Answer: No. Like the people of the whole country, the Chinese Communist Party will not allow Japan to retain an inch of Chinese territory.

Question: What, in your opinion, should be the main strategy and tactics to be followed in this "war of liberation"?

Answer: Our strategy should be to employ our main forces to operate over an extended and fluid front. To achieve success, the Chinese troops must conduct their warfare with a high degree of mobility on extensive battlefields, making swift advances and withdrawals, swift concentrations and dispersals. This means large scale mobile warfare, and not positional warfare depending exclusively on defense works with deep trenches, high fortresses and successive rows of defensive positions. It does not mean the abandonment of all the vital strategic points, which should be defended by positional warfare as long as profitable. But the pivotal strategy must be mobile warfare. Positional warfare is also necessary, but strategically it is auxiliary and secondary. Geographically the theatre of the war is so vast that it is possible for us to conduct mobile warfare most effectively. In the face of the vigorous actions of our forces, the Japanese army will have to be cautious. Its war-machine is ponderous and slow-moving, with limited efficiency. If we concentrate our forces on a narrow front for a defensive war of attrition, we would be throwing away the advantages of our geography and economic organization and repeating the mistake of Abyssinia. In the early period of the war, we must avoid any major decisive battles, and must first employ mobile warfare gradually to break the morale and combat effectiveness of the enemy troops.

Besides employing trained armies to carry on mobile warfare, we must organize great numbers of guerrilla units among the peasants. One should know that the anti-Japanese volunteer units in the three northeastern provinces are only a minor demonstration of the latent power of resistance that can be mobilized from the peasants of the whole country. The Chinese peasants have very great latent power; properly organized and directed, they can keep the Japanese army busy twenty-four hours a day and worry it to death. It must be remembered that the war will be fought in China, that is to say, the Japanese army will be entirely surrounded by the hostile Chinese people, it will be forced to move in all its provisions and guard them, it must use large numbers of troops to protect its lines of communications and constantly guard against attacks, and it needs large forces to garrison Manchuria and Japan as well.

In the course of the war, China will be able to capture many Japanese soldiers and seize many weapons and munitions with which to arm herself; at the same time China will win foreign aid to reinforce the equipment of her troops gradually. Therefore China will be able to conduct positional warfare in the latter period of the war and make positional attacks on the Japanese-occupied areas. Thus Japan's economy will crack under the strain of China's long resistance and the morale of the Japanese forces will break under the trial of innumerable battles. On the Chinese side, however, the growing latent power of resistance will be constantly brought into play and large numbers of revolutionary people will be pouring into the front lines to fight for their freedom. The combination of all these and other factors will enable us to make the final and decisive attacks on the fortifications and bases in the Japanese-occupied areas and drive the Japanese forces of aggression out of China.

The above views have been proved correct in the light of the experience of the ten months of war and will also be borne out in the future.

7. As far back as August 25, 1937, less than two months after the Lukouchiao Incident, the Central Committee of the Chinese Communist Party clearly pointed out in its "Resolution on the Present Situation and the Tasks of the Party":

The military provocation by the Japanese aggressors at Lukouchiao and their occupation of Peiping and Tientsin represent only the beginning of their large-scale invasion of China south of the Great Wall. They have already begun their national mobilization for war. Their propaganda that they have "no desire to aggravate the situation" is only a smokescreen for further attacks.

The resistance at Lukouchiao on July 7 marked the starting point of China's national War of Resistance.

Thus a new stage has opened in China's political situation, the stage of actual resistance. The stage of preparation for resistance is over. In the present stage the central task is to mobilize all the nation's forces for victory in the War of Resistance.

The key to victory in the war now lies in developing the resistance that has already begun into a war of total resistance by the whole nation. Only through such a war of total resistance can final victory be won.

The existence of serious weaknesses in the War of Resistance may lead to many setbacks, retreats, internal splits, betrayals, temporary and partial compromises and other such reverses. Therefore it should be realized that the war will be an arduous and protracted war. But we are confident that, through the efforts of our Party and the whole people, the resistance already started will sweep aside all obstacles and continue to advance and develop.

The above thesis, too, has been proved correct in the light of the experience of the ten months of war and will also be borne out in the future.

8.    Epistemologically speaking, the source of all erroneous views on war lies in idealist and mechanistic tendencies on the question. People with such tendencies are subjective and one-sided in their approach to problems. They either indulge in groundless and purely subjective talk, or, basing themselves upon a single aspect or a temporary manifestation, magnify it with similar subjectivity into the whole of the problem. But there are two categories of erroneous views, one comprising fundamental, and therefore consistent, errors which are hard to correct, and the other comprising accidental, and therefore temporary, errors which

are easy to correct. Since both are wrong, both need to be corrected. Therefore, only by opposing idealist and mechanistic tendencies and taking an objective and all-sided view in making a study of war can we draw correct conclusions on the question of war.

# THE BASIS OF THE PROBLEM

9. Why is the War of Resistance against Japan a protracted war? Why will the final victory be China's? What is the basis for these statements?

The war between China and Japan is not just any war, it is specifically a war of life and death between semi-colonial and semi-feudal China and imperialist Japan, fought in the Nineteen Thirties. Herein lies the basis of the whole problem. The two sides in the war have many contrasting features, which will be considered in turn below.

10. The Japanese side. First, Japan is a powerful imperialist country, which ranks first in the East in military, economic and political organizational power, and is one of the five or six foremost imperialist countries of the world. These are the basic factors in Japan's war of aggression. The inevitability of the war and the impossibility of quick victory for China are due to Japan's imperialist system and her great military, economic and political-organizational power. Secondly, however, the imperialist character of Japan's social economy determines the imperialist character of her war, a war that is retrogressive and barbarous. In the Nineteen Thirties, the internal and external contradictions of Japanese imperialism have driven her not only to embark on an adventurist war unparalleled in scale but also to approach her final collapse. In terms of social development, Japan is no longer a thriving country; the war will not lead to the prosperity sought by her ruling classes but to the very reverse, the doom of Japanese imperialism. This is what we mean by the retrogressive nature of Japan's war. It is this reactionary quality, coupled with the military-feudal character of Japanese imperialism, that gives rise to the peculiar barbarity of Japan's war. All of which will

arouse to the utmost the class antagonisms within Japan, the antagonism between the Japanese and the Chinese nations, and the antagonism between Japan and most other countries of the world. The reactionary and barbarous character of Japan's war constitutes the primary reason for her inevitable defeat. Thirdly, Japan's war is conducted on the basis of her great military, economic and political-organizational power, but at the same time it rests on an inadequate natural endowment. Japan's military, economic and political-organizational power is great but quantitatively inadequate. Japan is a comparatively small country, deficient in manpower and in military, financial and material resources, and she cannot stand a long war. Japan's rulers are endeavoring to resolve this difficulty through war, but again they will get the very reverse of what they desire; that is to say, the war they have launched to resolve this difficulty will eventually aggravate it and even exhaust Japan's original resources. Fourthly and lastly, while Japan can get international support from the fascist countries, the international opposition she is bound to encounter will be greater than her international support. This opposition will gradually grow and eventually not only cancel out the support but even bear down upon Japan herself. Such is the law that an unjust cause finds meager support, and such is the consequence of the very nature of Japan's war. To sum up, Japan's advantage lies in her great capacity to wage war, and her disadvantages lie in the reactionary and barbarous nature of her war, in the inadequacy of her manpower and material resources, and in her meager international support. These are the characteristics on the Japanese side.

11. The Chinese side. First, we are a semi-colonial and semi-feudal country. The Opium War, [6] the Taiping Revolution, [7] the Reform Movement of 1898, [8] the Revolution of 1911 [9] and the Northern Expedition [10] -- the revolutionary or reform movements which aimed at extricating

China from her semi-colonial and semi-feudal state -- all met with serious setbacks, and China remains a semi-colonial and semi-feudal country. We are still a weak country and manifestly inferior to the enemy in military, economic and political-organizational power. Here again one can find the basis for the inevitability of the war and the impossibility of quick victory for China. Secondly, however, China's liberation movement, with its cumulative development over the last hundred years, is now different from that of any previous period. Although the domestic and foreign forces opposing it have caused it serious setbacks, at the same time they have tempered the Chinese people. Although China today is not so strong as Japan militarily, economically, politically and culturally, yet there are factors in China more progressive than in any other period of her history. The Communist Party of China and the army under its leadership represent these progressive factors. It is on the basis of this progress that China's present war of liberation can be protracted and can achieve final victory. By contrast with Japanese imperialism, which is declining, China is a country rising like the morning sun. China's war is progressive, hence its just character. Because it is a just war, it is capable of arousing the nation to unity, of evoking the sympathy of the people in Japan and of winning the support of most countries in the world. Thirdly, and again by contrast with Japan, China is a very big country with vast territory, rich resources, a large population and plenty of soldiers, and is capable of sustaining a long war. Fourthly and lastly, there is broad international support for China stemming from the progressive and just character of her wet, which is again exactly the reverse of the meager support for Japan's unjust cause. To sum up, China's disadvantage lies in her military weakness, and her advantages lie in the progressive and just character of her war, her great size and her abundant international support. These are China's characteristics.

12. Thus it can be seen that Japan has great military, economic and political-organizational power, but that her war is reactionary and barbarous, her manpower and material resources are inadequate, and she is in an unfavorable position internationally. China, on the contrary, has less military, economic and political-organizational power, but she is in her era of progress, her war is progressive and just, she is moreover a big country, a factor which enables her to sustain a protracted war, and she will be supported by most countries. The above are the basic, mutually contradictory characteristics of the Sino-Japanese war. They have determined and are determining all the political policies and military strategies and tactics of the two sides; they have determined and are determining the protracted character of the war and its outcome, namely, that the final victory will go to China and not to Japan. The war is a contest between these characteristics. They will change in the course of the war, each according to its own nature; and from this everything else will follow. These characteristics exist objectively and are not invented to deceive people; they constitute all the basic elements of the war, and are not incomplete fragments; they permeate all major and minor problems on both sides and all stages of the war, and they are not matters of no consequence. If anyone forgets these characteristics in studying the Sino-Japanese war, he will surely go wrong; and even though some of his ideas win credence for a time and may seem right, they will inevitably be proved wrong by the course of the war. On the basis of these characteristics we shall now proceed to explain the problems to be dealt with.

# REFUTATION OF THE THEORY OF
# NATIONAL SUBJUGATION

13.   The theorists of national subjugation, who see nothing but the contrast between the enemy's strength and our weakness, used to say, "Resistance will mean subjugation," and now they are saying: "The continuance of the war spells subjugation." We shall not be able to convince them merely by stating that Japan, though strong; is small, while China, though weak, is large. They can adduce historical instances, such as the destruction of the Sung Dynasty by the Yuan and the destruction of the Ming Dynasty by the Ching, to prove that a small but strong country can vanquish a large but weak one and, moreover, that a backward country can vanquish an advanced one. If we say these events occurred long ago and do not prove the point, they can cite the British subjugation of India to prove that a small but strong capitalist country can vanquish a large but weak and backward country. Therefore, we have to produce other grounds before we can silence and convince all the subjugationists, and supply everyone engaged in propaganda with adequate arguments to persuade those who are still confused or irresolute and so strengthen their faith in the War of Resistance.

14.   What then are the grounds we should advance? The characteristics of the epoch. These characteristics are concretely reflected in Japan's retrogression and paucity of support and in China's progress and abundance of support.

15.   Our war is not just any war, it is specifically a war between China and Japan fought in the Nineteen Thirties. Our enemy, Japan, is first of all a moribund imperialist power; she is already in her era of decline and is not only different from Britain at the time of the subjugation of India, when British

capitalism was still in the era of its ascendancy, but also different from what she herself was at the time of World War I twenty years ago. The present war was launched on the eve of the general collapse of world imperialism and, above all, of the fascist countries; that is the very reason the enemy has launched this adventurist war, which is in the nature of a last desperate struggle. Therefore, it is an inescapable certainty that it will not be China but the ruling circles of Japanese imperialism which will be destroyed as a result of the war. Moreover, Japan has undertaken this war at a time when many countries have been or are about to be embroiled in war, when we are all fighting or preparing to fight against barbarous aggression, and China's fortunes are linked with those of most of the countries and peoples of the world. This is the root cause of the opposition Japan has aroused and will increasingly arouse among those countries and peoples.

16.   What about China? The China of today cannot be compared with the China of any other historical period. She is a semi-colony and a semi-feudal society, and she is consequently considered a weak country. But at the same time, China is historically in her era of progress; this is the primary reason for her ability to defeat Japan.

When we say that the War of Resistance against Japan is progressive, we do not mean progressive in the ordinary or general sense, nor do we mean progressive in the sense that the Abyssinian war against Italy, or the Taiping Revolution or the Revolution of 1911 were progressive, we mean progressive in the sense that China is progressive today. In what way is the China of today progressive? She is progressive because she is no longer a completely feudal country and because we already have some capitalism in China, we have a bourgeoisie and a proletariat, we have vast numbers of people who have awakened or are awakening, we have a Communist Party, we have a politically progressive army -- the Chinese Red Army led by the Communist Party -- and we have the tradition and the experience of many decades of revolution, and especially the experience of the seventeen years since the 'founding of the Chinese Communist Party. This experience has schooled the people and the political parties of China and forms the very basis for the present unity against Japan. If it is said that without the experience of 1905 the victory of 1917 would have been impossible in Russia, then we can also say that without the experience of the last seventeen years it would be impossible to win our War of Resistance. Such is the internal situation.

In the existing international situation, China is not isolated in the war, and this fact too is without precedent in history. In the past, China's wars, and India's too, were wars fought in isolation. It is only today that we meet with world-wide popular movements, extraordinary in breadth and depth, which have arisen or are arising and which are supporting China. The Russian Revolution of 1917 also received international support, and thus the Russian workers and peasants won; but that support was not so broad in scale and deep in nature as ours today. The popular movements in the world today are developing on a scale and with a depth that are unprecedented. The existence of the Soviet Union is a particularly vital factor in present-day international politics, and the Soviet Union will certainly support China with the greatest enthusiasm; there was nothing like this twenty years ago. All these factors have created and are creating important conditions indispensable to China's final victory Large-scale direct assistance is as yet lacking and will come only in the future, but China is progressive and is a big country, and these are the factors enabling her to protract the war and to promote as well as await international help.

17. There is the additional factor that while Japan is a small country with a small territory, few resources, a small population and a limited number of soldiers, China is a big country with vast territory, rich resources, a large population and plenty of soldiers, so that, besides the contrast between strength and weakness, there is the contrast between a small country, retrogression and meager support and a big country, progress and abundant support. This is the reason why China will never be subjugated. It follows from the contrast between strength and weakness that Japan can ride roughshod over China for a certain time and to a certain extent, that China must unavoidably travel a hard stretch of road, and that the War of Resistance will be a protracted war and not a war of quick decision; nevertheless, it follows from the other contrast -- a small country, retrogression and meager support versus a big country, progress and abundant support -- that Japan cannot ride roughshod over China indefinitely but is sure to meet final defeat, while China can never be subjugated but is sure to win final victory.

18. Why was Abyssinia vanquished? First, she was not only weak but also small. Second, she was not as progressive as China; she was an old country passing from the slave to the serf system, a country without any capitalism or bourgeois political parties, let alone a Communist Party, and with no army such as the Chinese army, let alone one like the Eighth Route Army. Third, she was unable to hold out and wait for international assistance and had to fight her war in isolation. Fourth, and most important of all, there were mistakes in the direction of her war against Italy. Therefore Abyssinia was subjugated. But there is still quite extensive guerrilla warfare in Abyssinia, which, if persisted in, will enable the Abyssinians to recover their country when the world situation changes.

19. If the subjugationists quote the history of the failure of liberation movements in modern China to prove their assertions first that "resistance will mean subjugation", and then that "the continuance of the war spells subjugation", here again our answer is, "Times are different." China herself, the internal situation in Japan and the international environment are all different now. It is a serious matter that Japan is stronger than before while China in her unchanged semi-colonial and semi-feudal position is still fairly weak. It is also a fact that for the time being Japan can still control her people at home and exploit international contradictions in order to invade China. But during a long war, these things are bound to change in the opposite direction. Such changes are not yet accomplished facts, but they will become so in future. The subjugationists dismiss this point. As for China, we already have new people, a new political party, a new army and a new policy of resistance to Japan, a situation very different from that of over a decade ago, and what is more, all these will inevitably make further progress. It is true that historically the liberation movements met with repeated setbacks with the result that China could not accumulate greater strength for the present War of Resistance -- this is a very painful historical lesson, and never again should we destroy any of our revolutionary forces. Yet even on the present basis, by exerting great efforts we can certainly forge ahead gradually and increase the strength of our resistance. All such efforts should converge on the great Anti-Japanese National United Front. As for international support, though direct and large-scale assistance is not yet in sight, it is in the making, the international situation being fundamentally different from before. The countless failures in the liberation movement of modern China had their subjective and objective causes, but the situation today is entirely different. Today, although there are many difficulties which make the War of Resistance arduous -- such as the enemy's strength and our weakness, and the fact that his difficulties are just starting,

while our own progress is far from sufficient -- nevertheless many favorable conditions exist for defeating the enemy; we need only add our subjective efforts, and we shall be able to overcome the difficulties and win through to victory. These are favorable conditions such as never existed before in any period of our history, and that is why the War of Resistance against Japan, unlike the liberation movements of the past, will not end in failure.

## COMPROMISE OR RESISTANCE?
## CORRUPTION OR PROGRESS?

20. It has been fully explained above that the theory of national subjugation is groundless. But there are many people who do not subscribe to this theory; they are honest patriots, who are nevertheless deeply worried about the present situation. Two things are worrying them, fear of a compromise with Japan and doubts about the possibility of political progress. These two vexing questions are being widely discussed and no key has been found to their solution. Let us now examine them.

21. As previously explained, the question of compromise has its social roots, and as long as these roots exist the question is bound to arise. But compromise will not avail. To prove the point, again we need only look for substantiation to Japan, China, and the international situation. First take Japan. At the very beginning of the War of Resistance, we estimated that the time would come when an atmosphere conducive to compromise would arise, in other words, that after occupying northern China, Kiangsu and Chekiang, Japan would probably resort to the scheme of inducing China to capitulate. True enough, she did resort to the scheme, but the crisis soon passed, one reason being that the enemy everywhere pursued a barbarous policy and practiced naked plunder. Had China capitulated, every Chinese would have become a slave without a country. The enemy's predatory policy, the policy of subjugating China, has two aspects, the material and the spiritual, both of which are being applied universally to all Chinese, not only to the people of the lower strata but also to members of the upper strata; of course the latter are treated a little more politely, but the difference is only one of degree, not of principle. In the main the enemy is transplanting into the

interior of China the same old measures he adopted in the three northeastern provinces. Materially, he is robbing the common people even of their food and clothing, making them cry out in hunger and cold; he is plundering the means of production, thus ruining and enslaving China's national industries. Spiritually, he is working to destroy the national consciousness of the Chinese people. Under the flag of the "Rising Sun" all Chinese are forced to be docile subjects, beasts of burden forbidden to show the slightest trace of Chinese national spirit. This barbarous enemy policy will be carried deeper into the interior of China. Japan with her voracious appetite is unwilling to stop the war. As was inevitable, the policy set forth in the Japanese cabinet's statement of January 6, 1938 [11] is still being obstinately carried out, which has enraged all strata of the Chinese people. This rage is engendered by the reactionary and barbarous character of Japan's war -- "there is no escape from fate", and hence an absolute hostility has crystallized. It is to be expected that on some future occasion the enemy will once again resort to the scheme of inducing China to capitulate and that certain subjugationists will again crawl out and most probably collude with certain foreign elements (to be found in Britain, the United States and France, and especially among the upper strata in Britain) as partners in crime. But the general trend of events will not permit capitulation; the obstinate and peculiarly barbarous character of Japan's war has decided this aspect of the question.

22.    Second, let us take China. There are three factors contributing to China's perseverance in the War of Resistance. In the first place, the Communist Party, which is the reliable force leading the people to resist Japan. Next, the Kuomintang, which depends on Britain and the United States and hence will not capitulate to Japan unless they tell it to. Finally, the other political parties and groups, most of which oppose compromise and support the War of Resistance. With unity among these

three, whoever compromises will be standing with the traitors, and anybody will have the right to punish him. All those unwilling to be traitors have no choice but to unite and carry on the War of Resistance to the end; therefore compromise can hardly succeed.

23. Third, take the international aspect. Except for Japan's allies and certain elements in the upper strata of other capitalist countries, the whole world is in favor of resistance, and not of compromise by China. This factor reinforces China's hopes. Today the people throughout the country cherish the hope that international forces will gradually give China increasing help. It is not a vain hope; the existence of the Soviet Union in particular encourages China in her War of Resistance. The socialist Soviet Union, now strong as never before; has always shared China's joys and sorrows. In direct contrast to all the members of the upper strata in the capitalist countries who seek nothing but profits, the Soviet Union considers it its duty to help all weak nations and all revolutionary wars. That China is not fighting! her war in isolation has its basis not only in international support in general but in Soviet support in particular. China and the Soviet Union are in close geographical proximity, which aggravates Japan's crisis and facilitates China's War of Resistance. Geographical proximity to Japan increases the difficulties of China's resistance. Proximity to the Soviet Union, on the other hand, is a favorable condition for the War of Resistance.

24. Hence we may conclude that the danger of compromise exists but can be overcome. Even if the enemy can modify his policy to some extent, he cannot alter it fundamentally. In China the social roots of compromise are present, but the opponents of compromise are in the majority. Internationally, also, some forces favor compromise, but the main forces favor resistance. The combination of these three

factors makes it possible to overcome the danger of compromise and persist to the end in the War of Resistance.

25.    Let us now answer the second question. Political progress at home and perseverance in the War of Resistance are inseparable. The greater the political progress, the more we can persevere in the war, and the more we persevere in the war, the greater the political progress. But, fundamentally, everything depends on our perseverance in the War of Resistance. The unhealthy phenomena in various fields under the Kuomintang regime are very serious, and the accumulation of these undesirable factors over the years has caused great anxiety and vexation among the broad ranks of our patriots. But there is no ground for pessimism, since experience in the War of Resistance has already proved that the Chinese people have made as much progress in the last ten months as in many years in the past. Although the cumulative effects of long years of corruption are seriously retarding the growth of the people's strength to resist Japan, thus reducing the extent of our victories and causing us losses in the war, yet the over-all situation in China, in Japan and in the world is such that the Chinese people cannot but make progress. This progress will be slow because of the factor of corruption, which impedes progress. Progress and the slow pace of progress are two characteristics of the present situation, and the second ill accords with the urgent needs of the war, which is a source of great concern to patriots. But we are in the midst of a revolutionary war, and revolutionary war is an antitoxin which not only eliminates the enemy's poison but also purges us of our own filth. Every just, revolutionary war is endowed with tremendous power, which can transform many things or clear the way for their transformation. The Sino-Japanese war will transform both China and Japan; provided China perseveres in the War of Resistance and in the united front, the old Japan will surely be transformed into a new Japan and the old China

into a new China, and people and everything else in both China and Japan will be transformed during and after the war. It is proper for us to regard the anti-Japanese war and our national reconstruction as interconnected. To say that Japan can also be transformed is to say that the war of aggression by her rulers will end in defeat and may lead to a revolution by the Japanese people. The day of triumph of the Japanese people's revolution will be the day Japan is transformed. All this is closely linked with China's War of Resistance and is a prospect we should take into account.

# THE THEORY OF NATIONAL SUBJUGATION IS WRONG AND THE THEORY OF QUICK VICTORY IS LIKEWISE WRONG

26. In our comparative study of the enemy and ourselves with respect to the basic contradictory characteristics, such as relative strength, relative size, progress or reaction, and the relative extent of support, we have already refuted the theory of national subjugation, and we have explained why compromise is unlikely and why political progress is possible. The subjugationists stress the contradiction between strength and weakness and puff it up until it becomes the basis of their whole argument on the question, neglecting all the other contradictions. Their preoccupation with the contrast in strength shows their one-sidedness, and their exaggeration of this one side of the matter into the whole shows their subjectivism. Thus, if one looks at the matter as a whole, it will be seen that they have no ground to stand on and are wrong. As for those who are neither subjugationists nor confirmed pessimists, but who are in a pessimistic frame of mind for the moment simply because they are confused by the disparity between our strength and that of the enemy at a given time and in certain respects or by the corruption in the country, we should point out to them that their approach also tends to be one-sided and subjective. But in their case correction is relatively easy; once they are alerted, they will understand, for they are patriots and their error is only momentary.

27. The exponents of quick victory are likewise wrong. Either they completely forget the contradiction between strength and weakness, remembering only the other contradictions, or they exaggerate China's advantages beyond all semblance of reality and beyond recognition, or they presumptuously take the balance of forces at one time and

place for the whole situation, as in the old saying, "A leaf before the eye shuts out Mount Tail" In a word, they lack the courage to admit that the enemy is strong while we are weak. They often deny this point and consequently deny one aspect of the truth. Nor do they have the courage to admit the limitations of our advantages, and thus they deny another aspect of the truth. The result is that they make mistakes, big and small, and here again it is subjectivism and one-sidedness that are doing the mischief. These friends have their hearts in the right place, and they, too, are patriots. But while "the gentlemen's aspirations are indeed lofty", their views are wrong, and to act according to them would certainly be to run into a brick wall. For if appraisal does not conform to reality, action cannot attain its objective; and to act notwithstanding would mean the army's defeat and the nation's subjugation, so that the result would be the same as with the defeatists. Hence this theory of quick victory will not do either.

28. Do we deny the danger of national subjugation? No, we do not. We recognize that China faces two possible prospects, liberation or subjugation, and that the two are in violent conflict. Our task is to achieve liberation and to avert subjugation. The conditions for liberation are China's progress, which is basic, the enemy's difficulties, and international support. We differ from the subjugationists. Taking an objective and all-sided view, we recognize the two possibilities of national subjugation and liberation, stress that liberation is the dominant possibility, point out the conditions for its achievement, and strive to secure them. The subjugationists, on the other hand, taking a subjective and one-sided view, recognize only one possibility, that of subjugation; they do not admit the possibility of liberation, and still less point out the conditions necessary for liberation or strive to secure them. Moreover, while acknowledging the tendency to compromise and the corruption, we see other tendencies and phenomena

which, we indicate, will gradually prevail and are already in violent conflict with the former; in addition, we point out the conditions necessary for the healthy tendencies and phenomena to prevail, and we strive to overcome the tendency to compromise and to change the state of corruption. Therefore, contrary to the pessimists, we are not at all down-hearted.

29. Not that we would not like a quick victory; everybody would be in favor of driving the "devils" out overnight. But we point out that, in the absence of certain definite conditions, quick victory is something that exists only in one's mind and not in objective reality, and that it is a mere illusion, a false theory. Accordingly, having made an objective and comprehensive appraisal of all the circumstances concerning both the enemy and ourselves, we point out that the only way to final victory is the strategy of protracted war, and we reject the groundless theory of quick victory. We maintain that we must strive to secure all the conditions indispensable to final victory, and the more fully and the earlier these conditions are secured, the surer we shall be of victory and the earlier we shall win it. We believe that only in this way can the course of the war be shortened, and we reject the theory of quick victory, which is just idle talk and an effort to get things on the cheap.

# WHY A PROTRACTED WAR?

30.  Let us now examine the problem of protracted war. A correct answer to the question "Why a protracted war?" can be arrived at only on the basis of all the fundamental contrasts between China and Japan. For instance, if we say merely that the enemy is a strong imperialist power while we are a weak semi-colonial and semi-feudal country, we are in danger of falling into the theory of national subjugation. For neither in theory nor in practice can a struggle become protracted by simply pitting the weak against the strong. Nor can it become protracted by simply pitting the big against the small, the progressive against the reactionary, or abundant support against meager support. The annexation of a small country by a big one or of a big country by a small one is a common occurrence. It often happens that a progressive country which is not strong is destroyed by a big, reactionary country, and the same holds for everything that is progressive but not strong. Abundant or meager support is an important but a subsidiary factor, and the degree of its effect depends upon the fundamental factors on both sides. Therefore when we say that the War of Resistance against Japan is a protracted war, our conclusion is derived from the interrelations of all the factors at work on both sides. The enemy is strong and we are weak, and the danger of subjugation is there. But in other respects the enemy has shortcomings and we have advantages. The enemy's advantage can be reduced and his shortcomings aggravated by our efforts. On the other hand, our advantages can be enhanced and our shortcoming remedied by our efforts. Hence, we can win final victory and avert subjugation, while the enemy will ultimately be defeated and will be unable to avert the collapse of his whole imperialist system.

31. Since the enemy has advantages only in one respect but shortcomings in all others and we have shortcomings in only one respect but advantages in all others, why has this produced not a balance, but, on the contrary, a superior position for him and an inferior position for us at the present time? Quite clearly, we cannot consider the question in such a formal way. The fact is that the disparity between the enemy's strength and our own is now so great that the enemy's shortcomings have not developed, and for the time being cannot develop, to a degree sufficient to offset his strength, while our advantages have not developed, and for the time being cannot develop, to a degree sufficient to compensate for our weakness. Therefore there can as yet be no balance, only imbalance.

32. Although our efforts in persevering in the War of Resistance and the united front have somewhat changed the enemy's strength and superiority as against our weakness and inferiority, there has as yet been no basic change. Hence during a certain stage of the war, to a certain degree the enemy will be victorious and we shall suffer defeat. But why is it that in this stage the enemy's victories and our defeats are definitely restricted in degree and cannot be transcended by complete victory or complete defeat? The reason is that, first, from the very beginning the enemy's strength and our weakness have been relative and not absolute, and that, second, our efforts in persevering in the War of Resistance and in the united front have further accentuated this relativeness. In comparison with the original situation, the enemy is still strong, but unfavorable factors have reduced his strength, although not yet to a degree sufficient to destroy his superiority, and similarly we are still weak, but favorable factors have compensated for our weakness, although not yet to a degree sufficient to transform our inferiority. Thus it turns out that the enemy is relatively strong and we are relatively weak, that the enemy is in a

relatively superior and we are in a relatively inferior position. On both sides, strength and weakness, superiority and inferiority, have never been absolute, and besides, our efforts in persevering in resistance to Japan and in the united front during the war have brought about further changes in the original balance of forces between us and the enemy. Therefore, in this stage the enemy's victory and our defeat are definitely restricted in degree, and hence the war becomes protracted.

33.   But circumstances are continually changing. In the course of the war, provided we employ correct military and political tactics, make no mistakes of principle and exert our best efforts, the enemy's disadvantages and China's advantages will both grow as the war is drawn out, with the inevitable result that there will be a continual change in the difference in comparative strength and hence in the relative position of the two sides. When a new stage is reached, a great change will take place in the balance of forces, resulting in the enemy's defeat and our victory.

34.   At present the enemy can still manage to exploit his strength, and our War of Resistance has not yet fundamentally weakened him. The insufficiency in his manpower and material resources is not yet such as to prevent his offensive; on the contrary, they can still sustain his offensive to a certain extent. The reactionary and barbarous nature of his war, a factor which intensifies both class antagonisms within Japan and the resistance of the Chinese nation, has not yet brought about a situation which radically impedes his advance. The enemy's international isolation is increasing but is not yet complete. In many countries which have indicated they will help us, the capitalists dealing in munitions and war materials and bent solely on profit are still furnishing Japan with large quantities of war supplies, [12] and their governments [13] are still reluctant to join the Soviet Union in practical sanctions against

Japan. From all this it follows that our War of Resistance cannot be won quickly and can only be a protracted war. As for China, although there has been some improvement with regard to her weakness in the military, economic, political and cultural spheres in the ten months of resistance, it is still a long way from what is required to prevent the enemy's offensive and prepare our counteroffensive. Moreover, quantitatively speaking, we have had to sustain certain losses. Although all the factors favorable to us are having a positive effect, it will not be sufficient to halt the enemy's offensive and to prepare for our counter-offensive unless we make an immense effort. Neither the abolition of corruption and the acceleration of progress at home, nor the curbing of the pro-Japanese forces and the expansion of the anti-Japanese forces abroad, are yet accomplished facts. From all this it follows that our war cannot be won quickly but can only be a protracted war.

# THE THREE STAGES OF THE PROTRACTED WAR

35. Since the Sino-Japanese war is a protracted one and final victory will belong to China, it can reasonably be assumed that this protracted war will pass through three stages. The first stage covers the period of the enemy's strategic offensive and our strategic defensive. The second stage will be the period of the enemy's strategic consolidation and our preparation for the counter-offensive. The third stage will be the period of our strategic counter-offensive and the enemy's strategic retreat. It is impossible to predict the concrete situation in the three stages, but certain main trends in the war may be pointed out in the light of present conditions. The objective course of events will be exceedingly rich and varied, with many twists and turns, and nobody can cast a horoscope for the Sino-Japanese war; nevertheless it is necessary for the strategic direction of the war to make a rough sketch of its trends. Although our sketch may not be in full accord with the subsequent facts and will be amended by them, it is still necessary to make it in order to give firm and purposeful strategic direction to the protracted war.

36. The first stage has not yet ended. The enemy's design is to occupy Canton, Wuhan and Lanchow and link up these three points. To accomplish this aim the enemy will have to use at least fifty divisions, or about one and a half million men, spend from one and a half to two years, and expend more than ten thousand million yen. In penetrating so deeply, he will encounter immense difficulties, with consequences disastrous beyond imagination. As for attempting to occupy the entire length of the Canton-Hankow Railway and the Sian-Lanchow Highway, he will have to fight perilous battles and even so may not fully accomplish his design. But in drawing up our operational plan we should base ourselves on the assumption

that the enemy may occupy the three points and even certain additional areas, as well as link them up, and we should make dispositions for a protracted war, so that even if he does so, we shall be able to cope with him. In this stage the form of fighting we should adopt is primarily mobile warfare, supplemented by guerrilla and positional warfare. Through the subjective errors of the Kuomintang military authorities, positional warfare was assigned the primary role in the first phase of this stage, but it is nevertheless supplementary from the point of view of the stage as a whole. In this stage, China has already built up a broad united front and achieved unprecedented unity. Although the enemy has used and will continue to use base and shameless means to induce China to capitulate in the attempt to realize his plan for a quick decision and to conquer the whole country without much effort, he has failed so far, nor is he likely to succeed in the future. In this stage, in spite of considerable losses, China will make considerable progress, which will become the main basis for her continued resistance in the second stage. In the present stage the Soviet Union has already given substantial aid to China. On the enemy side, there are already signs of flagging morale, and his army's momentum of attack is less in the middle phase of this stage than it was in the initial phase, and it will diminish still further in the concluding phase. Signs of exhaustion are beginning to appear in his finances and economy; war-weariness is beginning to set in among his people and troops; and within the clique at the helm of the war, "war frustrations" are beginning to manifest themselves and pessimism about the prospects of the war is growing.

37. The second stage may be termed one of strategic stalemate. At the tail end of the first stage, the enemy will be forced to fix certain terminal points to his strategic offensive owing to his shortage of troops and our firm resistance, and upon reaching them he will stop his strategic offensive and

enter the stage of safeguarding his occupied areas. In the second stage, the enemy will attempt to safeguard the occupied areas and to make them his own by the fraudulent method of setting up puppet governments, while plundering the Chinese people to the limit; but again he will be confronted with stubborn guerrilla warfare. Taking advantage of the fact that the enemy's rear is unguarded, our guerrilla warfare will develop extensively in the first stage, and many base areas will be established, seriously threatening the enemy's consolidation of the occupied areas, and so in the second stage there will still be widespread fighting. In this stage, our form; of fighting will be primarily guerrilla warfare, supplemented by mobile warfare. China will still retain a large regular army, but she will find it difficult to launch the strategic counter-offensive immediately because, on the one hand, the enemy will adopt a strategically defensive position in the big cities and along the main lines of communication under his occupation and, on the other hand, China will not yet be adequately equipped technically. Except for the troops engaged in frontal defense against the enemy, our forces will be switched in large numbers to the enemy's rear in comparatively dispersed dispositions, and, basing themselves on all the areas not actually occupied by the enemy and co-ordinating with the people's local armed forces, they will launch extensive, fierce guerrilla warfare against enemy-occupied areas, keeping the enemy on the move as far as possible in order to destroy him in mobile warfare, as is now being done in Shansi Province. The fighting in the second stage will be ruthless, and the country will suffer serious devastation. But the guerrilla warfare will be successful, and if it is well conducted the enemy may be able to retain only about one-third of his occupied territory, with the remaining two-thirds in our hands, and this will constitute a great defeat for the enemy and a great victory for China. By then the enemy-occupied territory as a whole will fall into three categories: first, the enemy base areas; second, our base areas for guerrilla warfare; and, third, the guerrilla areas contested by both sides. The duration of this stage will depend on the degree of change in the balance of forces between us and the enemy and on the changes in the international situation; generally speaking, we should be prepared to see this stage last a comparatively long time and to weather its hardships. It will be a very painful period for China; the two big problems will be economic difficulties and the disruptive activities of the traitors. The enemy will go all out to wreck China's united front, and the traitor organizations in all the occupied areas will merge into a so-called "unified government". Owing to the loss of big cities and the hardships of war, vacillating elements within our ranks will clamor for compromise, and pessimism will grow to a serious extent. Our tasks will then be to mobilize the whole people to unite as one man and carry on the war with unflinching perseverance, to broaden and consolidate the united front, sweep away all pessimism and ideas of compromise, promote the will to hard struggle and apply new wartime policies, and so to weather the hardships. In the second stage, we will have to call upon the whole country resolutely to maintain a united government, we will have to oppose splits and systematically improve fighting techniques, reform the armed forces, mobilize the entire people and prepare for the counter-offensive. The international situation will become still more unfavorable to Japan and the main international forces will incline towards giving more help to China, even though there may be talk of "realism" of the Chamberlain type which accommodates itself to fait accomplis. Japan's threat to Southeast Asia and Siberia will become greater, and there may even be another war. As regards Japan, scores of her divisions will be inextricably bogged down in China. Widespread guerrilla warfare and the people's anti-Japanese movement will wear down this big Japanese force, greatly reducing it and also disintegrating its morale by stimulating the growth of homesickness, war-weariness and even anti-war sentiment. Though it would be wrong to say that Japan will achieve no results at all in her plunder of China, yet, being short of capital and harassed by guerrilla warfare, she cannot possibly achieve rapid or substantial results. This second stage will be the transitional stage of the entire war; it will be the most trying period but also the pivotal one. Whether China becomes an independent country or is reduced to a colony will be determined not by the retention or loss of the big cities in the first stage but by the extent to which the whole nation exerts itself in the second. If we can persevere in the War of Resistance, in the united front and in the protracted war, China will in that stage gain the power to change from weakness to strength. It will be the second act in the three-act drama of China's War of Resistance. And through the efforts of the entire cast it will become possible to perform a most brilliant last act.

38. The third stage will be the stage of the counter-offensive to recover our lost territories. Their recovery will depend mainly upon the strength which China has built up in the preceding stage and which will continue to grow in the third stage. But China's strength alone will not be sufficient, and we shall also have to rely on the support of international forces and on the changes that will take place inside Japan, or otherwise we shall not be able to win; this adds to China's tasks in international propaganda and diplomacy. In the third stage, our war will no longer be one of strategic defensive, but will turn into a strategic counter-offensive manifesting itself in strategic offensives; and it will no longer be fought on strategically interior lines, but will shift gradually to strategically exterior lines. Not until we fight our way to the Yalu River can this war be considered over. The third stage will be the last in the protracted war, and when we talk of persevering in the war to the end, we mean going all the way through this stage. Our primary form of fighting will still be

mobile warfare, but positional warfare will rise to importance. While positional defense cannot be regarded as important in the first stage because of the prevailing circumstances, positional attack will become quite important in the third stage because of the changed conditions and the requirements of the task. In the third stage guerrilla warfare will again provide strategic support by supplementing mobile and positional warfare, but it will not be the primary form as in the second stage.

39. It is thus obvious that the war is protracted and consequently ruthless in nature. The enemy will not be able to gobble up the whole of China but will be able to occupy many places for a considerable time. China will not be able to oust the Japanese quickly, but the greater part of her territory will remain in her hands. Ultimately the enemy will lose and we will win, but we shall have a hard stretch of road to travel.

40. The Chinese people will become tempered in the course of this long and ruthless war. The political parties taking part in the war will also be steeled and tested. The united front must be persevered in; only by persevering in the united front can we persevere in the war; and only by persevering in the united front and in the war can we win final victory. Only thus can all difficulties be overcome. After travelling the hard stretch of road we shall reach the highway to victory. This is the natural logic of the war.

41. In the three stages the changes in relative strength will proceed along the following lines. In the first stage, the enemy is superior and we are inferior in strength. With regard to our inferiority we must reckon on changes of two different kinds from the eve of the War of Resistance to the end of this stage. The first kind is a change for the worse. China's original inferiority will be aggravated by war losses, namely, decreases

in territory, population, economic strength, military strength and cultural institutions. Towards the end of the first stage, the decrease will probably be considerable, especially on the economic side. This point will be exploited by some people as a basis for their theories of national subjugation and of compromise. But the second kind of change, the change for the better, must also be noted. It includes the experience gained in the war, the progress made by the armed forces, the political progress, the mobilization of the people, the development of culture in a new direction, the emergence of guerrilla warfare, the increase in international support, etc. What is on the downgrade in the first stage is the old quantity and the old quality, the manifestations being mainly quantitative. What is on the upgrade is the new quantity and the new quality, the manifestations being mainly qualitative. It is the second kind of change that provides a basis for our ability to fight a protracted war and win final victory.

42. In the first stage, changes of two kinds are also occurring on the enemy's side. The first kind is a change for the worse and manifests itself in hundreds of thousands of casualties, the drain on arms and ammunition, deterioration of troop morale, popular discontent at home, shrinkage of trade, the expenditure of over ten thousand million yen, condemnation by world opinion, etc. This trend also provides a basis for our ability to fight a protracted war and win final victory. But we must likewise reckon with the second kind of change on the enemy's side, a change for the better, that is, his expansion in territory, population and resources. This too is a basis for the protracted nature of our War of Resistance and the impossibility of quick victory, but at the same time certain people will use it as a basis for their theories of national subjugation and of compromise. However, we must take into account the transitory and partial character of this change for the better on the enemy's side. Japan is an imperialist power

heading for collapse, and her occupation of China's territory is temporary. The vigorous growth of guerrilla warfare in China will restrict her actual occupation to narrow zones. Moreover, her occupation of Chinese territory has created and intensified contradictions between Japan and other foreign countries. Besides, generally speaking, such occupation involves a considerable period in which Japan will make capital outlays without drawing any profits, as is shown by the experience in the three northeastern provinces. All of which again gives us a basis for demolishing the theories of national subjugation and of compromise and for establishing the theories of protracted war and of final victory.

43. In the second stage, the above changes on both sides will continue to develop. While the situation cannot be predicted in detail, on the whole Japan will continue on the downgrade and China on the upgrade. [14] For example, Japan's military and financial resources will be seriously drained by China's guerrilla warfare, popular discontent will grow in Japan, the morale of her troops will deteriorate further, and she will become more isolated internationally. As for China, she will make further progress in the political, military and cultural spheres and in the mobilization of the people; guerrilla warfare will develop further; there will be some new economic growth on the basis of the small industries and the widespread agriculture in the interior; international support will gradually increase; and the whole picture will be quite different from what it is now. This second stage may last quite a long time, during which there will be a great reversal in the balance of forces, with China gradually rising and Japan gradually declining. China will emerge from her inferior position, and Japan will lose her superior position; first the two countries will become evenly matched, and then their relative positions will be reversed. Thereupon, China will in general have completed her preparations for the strategic counter-offensive

and will enter the stage of the counter-offensive and the expulsion of the enemy. It should be reiterated that the change from inferiority to superiority and the completion of preparations for the counter-offensive will involve three things, namely, an increase in China's own strength, an increase in Japan's difficulties, and an increase in international support; it is the combination of all these forces that will bring about China's superiority and the completion of her preparations for the counter-offensive.

44. Because of the unevenness in China's political and economic development, the strategic counter-offensive of the third stage will not present a uniform and even picture throughout the country in its initial phase but will be regional in character, rising here and subsiding there. During this stage, the enemy will not relax his divisive tricks to break China's united front, hence the task of maintaining internal unity in China will become still more important, and we shall have to ensure that the strategic counter-offensive does not collapse halfway through internal dissension. In this period the international situation will become very favorable to China. China's task will be to take advantage of it in order to attain complete liberation and establish an independent democratic state, which at the same time will mean helping the world anti-fascist movement.

45. China moving from inferiority to parity and then to superiority, Japan moving from superiority to parity and then to inferiority; China moving from the defensive to stalemate and then to the counter-offensive, Japan moving from the offensive to the safeguarding of her gains and then to retreat -- such will be the course of the Sino-Japanese war and its inevitable trend.

46. Hence the questions and the conclusions are as follows: Will China be subjugated? The answer is; No, she will

not be subjugated, but will win final victory. Can China win quickly? The answer is, No, she cannot win quickly, and the war must be a protracted one. Are these conclusions correct? I think they are.

47.   At this point, the exponents of national subjugation and of compromise will again rush in and say, "To move from inferiority to parity China needs a military and economic power equal to Japan's, and to move from parity to superiority she will need a military and economic power greater than Japan's. But this is impossible, hence the above conclusions are not correct."

48.   This is the so-called theory that "weapons decide everything", [15] which constitutes a mechanical approach to the question of war and a subjective and one-sided view. Our view is opposed to this; we see not only weapons but also people. Weapons are an important factor in war, but not the decisive factor; it is people, not things, that are decisive. The contest of strength is not only a contest of military and economic power, but also a contest of human power and morale. Military and economic power is necessarily wielded by people. If the great majority of the Chinese, of the Japanese and of the people of other countries are on the side of our War of Resistance against Japan, how can Japan's military and economic power, wielded as it is by a small minority through coercion, count as superiority? And if not, then does not China, though wielding relatively inferior military and economic power, become the superior? There is no doubt that China will gradually grow in military and economic power, provided she perseveres in the War of Resistance and in the united front. As for our enemy, weakened as he will be by the long war and by internal and external contradictions, his military and economic power is bound to change in the reverse direction. In these circumstances, is there any reason why China cannot become

the superior? And that is not all. Although we cannot as yet count the military and economic power of other countries as being openly and to any great extent on our side, is there any reason why we will not be able to do so in the future? If Japan's enemy is not just China, if in future one or more other countries make open use of their considerable military and economic power defensively or offensively against Japan and openly help us, then will not our superiority be still greater? Japan is a small country, her war is reactionary and barbarous, and she will become more and more isolated internationally; China is a large country, her war is progressive and just, and she will enjoy more and more support internationally. Is there any reason why the long-term development of these factors should not definitely change the relative position between the enemy and ourselves?

49. The exponents of quick victory, however, do not realize that war is a contest of strength, and that before a certain change has taken place in the relative strength of the belligerents, there is no basis for trying to fight strategically decisive battles and shorten the road to liberation. Were their ideas to be put into practice, we should inevitably run our heads into a brick wall. Or perhaps they are just talking for their own pleasure without really intending to put their ideas into practice. In the end Mr. Reality will come and pour a bucket of cold water over these chatterers, showing them up as mere windbags who want to get things on the cheap, to have gains without pains. We have had this kind of idle chatter before and we have it now, though not very much so far; but there may be more as the war develops into the stage of stalemate and then of counter-offensive. But in the meantime, if China's losses in the first stage are fairly heavy and the second stage drags on very long, the theories of national subjugation and of compromise will gain great currency.

Therefore, our fire should be directed mainly against them and only secondarily against the idle chatter about quick victory.

50. That the war will be protracted is certain, but nobody can predict exactly how many months or years it will last, as this depends entirely upon the degree of the change in the balance of forces. All those who wish to shorten the war have no alternative but to work hard to increase our own strength and reduce that of the enemy. Specifically, the only way is to strive to win more battles and wear down the enemy's forces, develop guerrilla warfare to reduce enemy-occupied territory to a minimum, consolidate and expand the united front to rally the forces of the whole nation, build up new armies and develop new war industries, promote political, economic and cultural progress, mobilize the workers, peasants, businessmen, intellectuals and other sections of the people, disintegrate the enemy forces and win over their soldiers, carry on international propaganda to secure foreign support, and win the support of the Japanese people and other oppressed peoples. Only by doing all this can we reduce the duration of the war. There is no magic short-cut.

# A WAR OF JIG-SAW PATTERN

51. We can say with certainty that the protracted War of Resistance against Japan will write a splendid page unique in the war history of mankind. One of the special features of this war is the interlocking "jig-saw" pattern which arises from such contradictory factors as the barbarity of Japan and her shortage of troops on the one hand, and the progressiveness of China and the extensiveness of her territory on the other. There have been other wars of jig-saw pattern in history, the three years' civil war in Russia after the October Revolution being a case in point. But what distinguishes this war in China is its especially protracted and extensive character, which will set a record in history. Its jig-saw pattern manifests itself as follows.

52. Interior and exterior lines. The anti-Japanese war as a whole is being fought on interior lines; but as far as the relation between the main forces and the guerrilla units is concerned, the former are on the interior lines while the latter are on the exterior lines, presenting a remarkable spectacle of pincers around the enemy. The same can be said of the relationship between the various guerrilla areas. From its own viewpoint each guerrilla area is on interior lines and the other areas are on exterior lines; together they form many battle fronts, which hold the enemy in pincers. In the first stage of the war, the regular army operating strategically on interior lines is withdrawing, but the guerrilla units operating strategically on exterior lines will advance with great strides over wide areas to the rear of the enemy -- they will advance even more fiercely in the second stage -- thereby presenting a remarkable picture of both withdrawal and advance.

53. Possession and non-possession of a rear area. The main forces, which extend the front lines to the outer limits of

the enemy's occupied areas, are operating from the rear area of the country as a whole. The guerrilla units, which extend the battle lines into the enemy rear, are separated from the rear area of the country as a whole. But each guerrilla area has a small rear of its own, upon which it relies to establish its fluid battle lines. The case is different with the guerrilla detachments which are dispatched by a guerrilla area for short-term operations in the rear of the enemy in the same area; such detachments have no rear, nor do they have a battle line. "Operating without a rear area" is a special feature of revolutionary war in the new era, wherever a vast territory, a progressive people, and an advanced political party and army are to be found; there is nothing to fear but much to gain from it, and far from having doubts about it we should promote it.

54. Encirclement and counter-encirclement. Taking the war as a whole, there is no doubt that we are strategically encircled by the enemy because he is on the strategic offensive and operating on exterior lines while we are on the strategic defensive and operating on interior lines. This is the first form of enemy encirclement. We on our part can encircle one or more of the enemy columns advancing on us along separate routes, because we apply the policy of fighting campaigns and battles from tactically exterior lines by using numerically preponderant forces against these enemy columns advancing on us from strategically exterior lines. This is the first form of our counter-encirclement of the enemy. Next, if we consider the guerrilla base areas in the enemy's rear, each area taken singly is surrounded by the enemy on all sides, like the Wutai Mountains, or on three sides, like the northwestern Shansi area. This is the second form of enemy encirclement. However, if one considers all the guerrilla base areas together and in their relation to the positions of the regular forces, one can see that we in turn surround a great many enemy forces. In Shansi Province, for instance, we have surrounded the Tatung-Puchow

Railway on three sides (the east and west flanks and the southern end) and the city of Taiynan on all sides; and there are many similar instances in Hopei and Shantung Provinces. This is the second form of our counter-encirclement of the enemy. Thus there are two forms of encirclement by the enemy forces and two forms of encirclement by our own -- rather like a game of weichi. [16] Campaigns and battles fought by the two sides resemble the capturing of each other's pieces, and the establishment of enemy strongholds (such as Taiyuan) and our guerrilla base areas (such as the Wutai Mountains) resembles moves to dominate spaces on the board. If the game of weichi is extended to include the world, there is yet a third form of encirclement as between us and the enemy, namely, the interrelation between the front of aggression and the front of peace. The enemy encircles China, the Soviet Union, France and Czechoslovakia with his front of aggression, while we counter-encircle Germany, Japan and Italy with our front of peace. But our encirclement, like the hand of Buddha, will turn into the Mountain of Five Elements lying athwart the Universe, and the modern Sun Wu-kungs [17] -- the fascist aggressors -- will finally be buried underneath it, never to rise again. Therefore, if on the international plane we can create an anti-Japanese front in the Pacific region, with China as one strategic unit, with the Soviet Union and other countries which may join it as other strategic units, and with the Japanese people's movement as still another strategic unit, and thus form a gigantic net from which the fascist Sun Wu-kungs can kind no escape, then that will be our enemy's day of doom. Indeed, the day when this gigantic net is formed will undoubtedly be the day of the complete overthrow of Japanese imperialism. We are not jesting; this is the inevitable trend of the war.

55. Big areas and little areas. There is a possibility that the enemy will occupy the greater part of Chinese territory south of the Great Wall, and only the smaller part will be kept

intact. That is one aspect of the situation. But within this greater part, which does not include the three northeastern provinces, the enemy can actually hold only the big cities, the main lines of communication and some of the plains -- which may rank first in importance, but will probably constitute only the smaller part of the occupied territory in size and population, while the greater part will be taken up by the guerrilla areas that will grow up everywhere. That is another aspect of the situation. If we go beyond the provinces south of the Great Wall and include Mongolia, Sinkiang, Chinghai and Tibet, then the unoccupied area will constitute the greater part of China's territory, and the enemy-occupied area will become the smaller part, even with the three northeastern provinces. That is yet another aspect of the situation. The area kept intact is undoubtedly important, and we should devote great efforts to developing it, not only politically, militarily and economically but, what is also important, culturally. The enemy has transformed our former cultural centers into culturally backward areas, and we on our part must transform the former culturally backward areas into cultural centers. At the same time, the work of developing extensive guerrilla areas behind the enemy lines is also extremely important, and we should attend to every aspect of this work, including the cultural. All in all, big pieces of China's territory, namely, the rural areas, will be transformed into regions of progress and light, while the small pieces, namely, the enemy-occupied areas and especially the big cities, will temporarily become regions of backwardness and darkness.

56. Thus it can be seen that the protracted and far-flung War of Resistance against Japan is a war of a jig-saw pattern militarily, politically, economically and culturally. It is a marvelous spectacle in the annals of war, a heroic undertaking by the Chinese nation, a magnificent and earth-shaking feat. This war will not only affect China and Japan, strongly

impelling both to advance, but will also affect the whole world, impelling all nations, especially the oppressed nations such as India, to march forward. Every Chinese should consciously throw himself into this war of a jig-saw pattern, for this is the form of war by which the Chinese nation is liberating itself, the special form of war of liberation waged by a big semi-colonial country in the Nineteen Thirties and the Nineteen Forties.

## FIGHTING FOR PERPETUAL PEACE

57. The protracted nature of China's anti-Japanese war is inseparably connected with the fight for perpetual peace in China and the whole world. Never has there been a historical period such as the present in which war is so close to perpetual peace. For several thousand years since the emergence of classes, the life of mankind has been full of wars; each nation has fought countless wars, either internally or with other nations. In the imperialist epoch of capitalist society, wars are waged on a particularly extensive scale and with a peculiar ruthlessness. The first great imperialist war of twenty years ago was the first of its kind in history, but not the last. Only the war which has now begun comes close to being the final war, that is, comes close to the perpetual peace of mankind. By now one-third of the world's population has entered the war. Look! Italy, then Japan; Abyssinia, then Spain, then China. The population of the countries at war now amounts to almost 600 million, or nearly a third of the total population of the world. The characteristics of the present war are its uninterruptedness and its proximity to perpetual peace. Why is it uninterrupted? After attacking Abyssinia, Italy attacked Spain, and Germany joined in; then Japan attacked China. What will come next? Undoubtedly Hitler will fight the great powers. "Fascism is war" [18] -- this is perfectly true. There will be no interruption in the development of the present war into a world war; mankind will not be able to avoid the calamity of war. Why then do we say the present war is near to perpetual peace? The present war is the result of the development of the general crisis of world capitalism which began with World War I; this general crisis is driving the capitalist countries into a new war and, above all, driving the fascist countries into new war adventures. This war, we can foresee, will not save capitalism, but will hasten its collapse. It will be greater in scale and more

ruthless than the war of twenty years ago, all nations will inevitably be drawn in, it will drag on for a very long time, and mankind will suffer greatly. But, owing to the existence of the Soviet Union and the growing political consciousness of the people of the world, great revolutionary wars will undoubtedly emerge from this war to oppose all counter-revolutionary wars, thus giving this war the character of a struggle for perpetual peace. Even if later there should be another period of war, perpetual world peace will not be far off. Once man has eliminated capitalism, he will attain the era of perpetual peace, and there will be no more need for war. Neither armies, nor warships, nor military aircraft, nor poison gas will then be needed. Thereafter and for all time, mankind will never again know war. The revolutionary wars which have already begun are part of the war for perpetual peace. The war between China and Japan, two countries which have a combined population of over 500 million, will take an important place in this war for perpetual peace, and out of it will come the liberation of the Chinese nation. The liberated new China of the future will be inseparable from the liberated new world of the future. Hence our War of Resistance against Japan takes on the character of a struggle for perpetual peace.

58. History shows that wars are divided into two kinds, just and unjust. All wars that are progressive are just, and all wars that impede progress are unjust. We Communists oppose all unjust wars that impede progress, but we do not oppose progressive, just wars. Not only do we Communists not oppose just wars, we actively participate in them. As for unjust wars, World War I is an instance in which both sides fought for imperialist interests; therefore the Communists of the whole world firmly opposed that war. The way to oppose a war of this kind is to do everything possible to prevent it before it breaks out and, once it breaks out, to oppose war with war, to oppose unjust war with just war, whenever possible. Japan's war is an

unjust war that impedes progress, and the peoples of the world, including the Japanese people, should oppose it and are opposing it. In our country the people and the government, the Communist Party and the Kuomintang, have all raised the banner of righteousness in the national revolutionary war against aggression. Our war is sacred and just, it is progressive and its aim is peace. The aim is peace not just in one country but throughout the world, not just temporary but perpetual peace. To achieve this aim we must wage a life-and-death struggle, be prepared for any sacrifice, persevere to the end and never stop short of the goal. However great the sacrifice and however long the time needed to attain it, a new world of perpetual peace and brightness already lies clearly before us. Our faith in waging this war is based upon the new China and the new world of perpetual peace and brightness for which we are striving. Fascism and imperialism wish to perpetuate war, but we wish to put an end to it in the not too distant future. The great majority of mankind should exert their utmost efforts for this purpose. The 450 million people of China constitute one quarter of the world's population, and if by their concerted efforts they overthrow Japanese imperialism and create a new China of freedom and equality, they will most certainly be making a tremendous contribution to the struggle for perpetual world peace. This is no vain hope, for the whole world is approaching this point in the course of its social and economic development, and provided that the majority of mankind work together, our goal will surely be attained in several decades.

# MAN'S DYNAMIC ROLE IN WAR

59. We have so far explained why the war is a protracted war and why the final victory will be China's, and in the main dealt with what protracted war is and what it is not. Now we shall turn to the question of what to do and what not to do. How to conduct protracted war and how to win the final victory? These are the questions answered below. We shall therefore successively discuss the following problems: man's dynamic role in war, war and politics, political mobilization for the War of Resistance, the object of war, offence within defense, quick decisions within a protracted war, exterior lines within interior lines, initiative, flexibility, planning, mobile warfare, guerrilla warfare' positional warfare, war of annihilation, war of attrition, the possibilities of exploiting the enemy's mistakes, the question of decisive engagements in the anti-Japanese war, and the army and the people as the foundation of victory. Let us start with the problem of man's dynamic role.

60. When we say we are opposed to a subjective approach to problems, we mean that we must oppose ideas which are not based upon or do not correspond to objective facts, because such ideas are fanciful and fallacious and will lead to failure if acted on. But whatever is done has to be done by human beings; protracted war and final victory will not come about without human action. For such action to be effective there must be people who derive ideas, principles or views from the objective facts, and put forward plans, directives, policies, strategies and tactics. Ideas, etc. are subjective, while deeds or actions are the subjective translated into the objective, but both represent the dynamic role peculiar to human beings. We term this kind of dynamic role "man's conscious dynamic role", and it is a characteristic that

distinguishes man from all other beings. All ideas based upon and corresponding to objective facts are correct ideas, and all deeds or actions based upon correct ideas are correct actions. We must give full scope to these ideas and actions, to this dynamic role. The anti-Japanese war is being waged to drive out imperialism and transform the old China into a new China; this can be achieved only when the whole Chinese people are mobilized and full scope is given to their conscious dynamic role in resisting Japan. If we just sit by and take no action, only subjugation awaits us and there will be neither protracted war nor final victory.

61. It is a human characteristic to exercise a conscious dynamic role. Man strongly displays this characteristic in war. True, victory or defeat in war is decided by the military, political, economic and geographical conditions on both sides, the nature of the war each side is waging and the international support each enjoys, but it is not decided by these alone; in themselves, all these provide only the possibility of victory or defeat but do not decide the issue. To decide the issue, subjective effort must be added, namely, the directing and waging of war, man's conscious dynamic role in war.

62. In seeking victory, those who direct a war cannot overstep the limitations imposed by the objective conditions; within these limitations, however, they can and must play a dynamic role in striving for victory. The stage of action for commanders in a war must be built upon objective possibilities, but on that stage they can direct the performance of many a drama, full of sound and color, power and grandeur. Given the objective material foundations, the commanders in the anti-Japanese war should display their prowess and marshal all their forces to crush the national enemy, transform the present situation in which our country and society are suffering from aggression and oppression, and create a new China of freedom

and equality; here is where our subjective faculties for directing war can and must be exercised. We do not want any of our commanders in the war to detach himself from the objective conditions and become a blundering hothead, but we decidedly want every commander to become a general who is both bold and sagacious. Our commanders should have not only the boldness to overwhelm the enemy but also the ability to remain masters of the situation throughout the changes and vicissitudes of the entire war. Swimming in the ocean of war, they must not flounder but make sure of reaching the opposite shore with measured strokes. Strategy and tactics, as the laws for directing war, constitute the art of swimming in the ocean of war.

## WAR AND POLITICS

63. "War is the continuation of politics." In this sense war is politics and war itself is a political action; since ancient times there has never been a war that did not have a political character. The anti-Japanese war is a revolutionary war waged by the whole nation, and victory is inseparable from the political aim of the war -- to drive out Japanese imperialism and build a new China of freedom and equality -- inseparable from the general policy of persevering in the War of Resistance and in the united front, from the mobilization of the entire people, and from the political principles of the unity between officers and men, the unity between army and people and the disintegration of the enemy forces, and inseparable from the effective application of united front policy, from mobilization on the cultural front, and from the efforts to win international support and the support of the people inside Japan. In a word, war cannot for a single moment be separated from politics. Any tendency among the anti-Japanese armed forces to belittle politics by isolating war from it and advocating the idea of war as an absolute is wrong and should be corrected.

64. But war has its own particular characteristics and in this sense it cannot be equated with politics in general. "War is the continuation of politics by other . . . means." [19] When politics develops to a certain stage beyond which it cannot proceed by the usual means, war breaks out to sweep the obstacles from the way. For instance, the semi-independent status of China is an obstacle to the political growth of Japanese imperialism, hence Japan has unleashed a war of aggression to sweep away that obstacle. What about China? Imperialist oppression has long been an obstacle to China's bourgeois-democratic revolution, hence many wars of

liberation have been waged in the effort to sweep it away. Japan is now using war for the purpose of oppressing China and completely blocking the advance of the Chinese revolution, and therefore China is compelled to wage the War of Resistance in her determination to sweep away this obstacle. When the obstacle is removed, our political aim will be attained and the war concluded. But if the obstacle is not completely swept away, the war will have to continue till the aim is fully accomplished. Thus anyone who seeks a compromise before the task of the anti-Japanese war is fulfilled is bound to fail, because even if a compromise were to occur for one reason or another, the war would break out again, since the broad masses of the people would certainly not submit but would continue the war until its political objective was achieved. It can therefore be said that politics is war without bloodshed while war is politics with bloodshed.

65. From the particular characteristics of war there arise a particular set of organizations, a particular series of methods and a particular kind of process. The organizations are the armed forces and everything that goes with them. The methods are the strategy and tactics for directing war. The process is the particular form of social activity in which the opposing armed forces attack each other or defend themselves against one another, employing strategy and tactics favorable to themselves and unfavorable to the enemy. Hence war experience is a particular kind of experience. All who take part in war must rid themselves of their customary ways and accustom themselves to war before they can win victory.

## POLITICAL MOBILIZATION FOR
## THE WAR OF RESISTANCE

66. A national revolutionary war as great as ours cannot be won without extensive and thoroughgoing political mobilization. Before the anti-Japanese war there was no political mobilization for resistance to Japan, and this was a great drawback, as a result of which China has already lost a move to the enemy. After the war began, political mobilization was very far from extensive, let alone thoroughgoing. It was the enemy's gunfire and the bombs dropped by enemy aeroplanes that brought news of the war to the great majority of the people. That was also a kind of mobilization, but it was done for us by the enemy, we did not do it ourselves. Even now the people in the more remote regions beyond the noise of the guns are carrying on quietly as usual. This situation must change, or otherwise we cannot win in our life-and-death struggle. We must never lose another move to the enemy; on the contrary, we must make full use of this move, political mobilization, to get the better of him. This move is crucial; it is indeed of primary importance, while our inferiority in weapons and other things is only secondary. The mobilization of the common people throughout the country will create a vast sea in which to drown the enemy, create the conditions that will make up for our inferiority in arms and other things, and create the prerequisites for overcoming every difficulty in the war. To win victory, we must persevere in the War of Resistance, in the united front and in the protracted war. But all these are inseparable from the mobilization of the common people. To wish for victory and yet neglect political mobilization is like wishing to "go south by driving the chariot north", and the result would inevitably be to forfeit victory.

67. What does political mobilization mean? First, it means telling the army and the people about the political aim of the

war. It is necessary for every soldier and civilian to see why the war must be fought and how it concerns him. The political aim of the war is "to drive out Japanese imperialism and build a new China of freedom and equality"; we must proclaim this aim to everybody, to all soldiers and civilians, before we can create an anti-Japanese upsurge and unite hundreds of millions as one man to contribute their all to the war. Secondly, it is not enough merely to explain the aim to them; the steps and policies for its attainment must also be given, that is, there must be a political program. We already have the Ten-Point Program for Resisting Japan and Saving the Nation and also the Program of Armed Resistance and National Reconstruction; we should popularize both of them in the army and among the people and mobilize everyone to carry them out. Without a clear-cut, concrete political program it is impossible to mobilize all the armed forces and the whole people to carry the war against Japan through to the end. Thirdly, how should we mobilize them? By word of mouth, by leaflets and bulletins, by newspapers, books and pamphlets, through plays and films, through schools, through the mass organizations and through our cadres. What has been done so far in the Kuomintang areas is only a drop in the ocean, and moreover it has been done in a manner ill-suited to the people's tastes and in a spirit uncongenial to them; this must be drastically changed. Fourthly, to mobilize once is not enough; political mobilization for the War of Resistance must be continuous. Our job is not to recite our political program to the people, for nobody will listen to such recitations; we must link the political mobilization for the war with developments in the war and with the life of the soldiers and the people, and make it a continuous movement. This is a matter of immense importance on which our victory in the war primarily depends.

# THE OBJECT OF WAR

68. Here we are not dealing with the political aim of war; the political aim of the War of Resistance against Japan has been defined above as "to drive out Japanese imperialism and build a new China of freedom and equality". Here we are dealing with the elementary object of war, war as "politics with bloodshed", as mutual slaughter by opposing armies. The object of war is specifically "to preserve oneself and destroy the enemy" (to destroy the enemy means to disarm him or "deprive him of the power to resist", and does not mean to destroy every member of his forces physically). In ancient warfare, the spear and the shield were used, the spear to attack and destroy the enemy, and the shield to defend and preserve oneself To the present day, all weapons are still an extension of the spear and the shield. The bomber, the machine-gun, the long-range gun and poison gas are developments of the spear, while the air-raid shelter, the steel helmet, the concrete fortification and the gas mask are developments of the shield. The tank is a new weapon combining the functions of both spear and shield. Attack is the chief means of destroying the enemy, but defense cannot be dispensed with. In attack the immediate object is to destroy the enemy, but at the same time it is self-preservation, because if the enemy is not destroyed, you will be destroyed. In defense the immediate object is to preserve yourself, but at the same time defense is a means of supplementing attack or preparing to go over to the attack. Retreat is in the category of defense and is a continuation of defense, while pursuit is a continuation of attack. It should be pointed out that destruction of the enemy is the primary object of war and self-preservation the secondary, because only by destroying the enemy in large numbers can one effectively preserve oneself. Therefore attack, the chief means of destroying the enemy, is primary, while defense, a

supplementary means of destroying the enemy and a means of self-preservation, is secondary. In actual warfare the chief role is played by defense much of the time and by attack for the rest of the time, but if war is taken as a whole, attack remains primary.

69. How do we justify the encouragement of heroic sacrifice in war? Does it not contradict "self-preservation"? No, it does not; sacrifice and self-preservation are both opposite and complementary to each other. War is politics with bloodshed and exacts a price, sometimes an extremely high price. Partial and temporary sacrifice (non-preservation) is incurred for the sake of general and permanent preservation. This is precisely why we say that attack, which is basically a means of destroying the enemy, also has the function of self-preservation. It is also the reason why defense must be accompanied by attack and should not be defense pure and simple.

70. The object of war, namely, the preservation of oneself and the destruction of the enemy, is the essence of war and the basis of all war activities, an essence which pervades all war activities, from the technical to the strategic. The object of war is the underlying principle of war, and no technical, tactical, or strategic concepts or principles can in any way depart from it. What for instance is meant by the principle of "taking cover and making full use of fire-power" in shooting? The purpose of the former is self-preservation, of the latter the destruction of the enemy. The former gives rise to such techniques as making use of the terrain and its features, advancing in spurts, and spreading out in dispersed formation. The latter gives rise to other techniques, such as clearing the field of fire and organizing a fire-net. As for the assault force, the containing force and the reserve force in a tactical operation, the first is for annihilating the enemy, the second for preserving oneself, and

the third is for either purpose according to circumstances -- either for annihilating the enemy (in which case it reinforces the assault force or serves as a pursuit force), or for self-preservation (in which case it reinforces the containing force or serves as a covering force). Thus, no technical, tactical, or strategic principles or operations can in any way depart from the object of war, and this object pervades the whole of a war and runs through it from beginning to end.

71. In directing the anti-Japanese war, leaders at the various levels must lose sight neither of the contrast between the fundamental factors on each side nor of the object of this war. In the course of military operations these contrasting fundamental factors unfold themselves in the struggle by each side to preserve itself and destroy the other. In our war we strive in every engagement to win a victory, big or small, and to disarm a part of the enemy and destroy a part of his men and matériel. We must accumulate the results of these partial destructions of the enemy into major strategic victories and so achieve the final political aim of expelling the enemy, protecting the motherland and building a new China.

# OFFENSE WITHIN DEFENSE, QUICK DECISIONS WITHIN A PROTRACTED WAR, EXTERIOR LINES WITHIN INTERIOR LINES

72. Now let us examine the specific strategy of the War of Resistance against Japan. We have already said that our strategy for resisting Japan is that of protracted war, and indeed this is perfectly right. But this strategy is general, not specific. Specifically, how should the protracted war be conducted? We shall now discuss this question. Our answer is as follows. In the first and second stages of the war, i.e., in the stages of the enemy's offensive and preservation of his gains, we should conduct tactical offensives within the strategic defensive, campaigns and battles of quick decision within the strategically protracted war, and campaigns and battles on exterior lines within strategically interior lines. In the third stage, we should launch the strategic counter-offensive.

73. Since Japan is a strong imperialist power and we are a weak semi-colonial and semi-feudal country, she has adopted the policy of the strategic offensive while we are on the strategic defensive. Japan is trying to execute the strategy of a war of quick decision; we should consciously execute the strategy of protracted war. Japan is using dozens of army divisions of fairly high combat effectiveness (now numbering thirty) and part of her navy to encircle and blockade China from both land and sea, and is using her air force to bomb China. Her army has already established a long front stretching from Paotow to Hangchow and her navy has reached Fukien and Kwangtung; thus exterior-line operations have taken shape on a vast scale. On the other hand, we are in the position of operating on interior lines. All this is due to the fact that the

enemy is strong while we are weak. This is one aspect of the situation.

74. But there is another and exactly opposite aspect. Japan, though strong, does not have enough soldiers. China, though weak, has a vast territory, a large population and plenty of soldiers. Two important consequences follow. First, the enemy, employing his small forces against a vast country, can only occupy some big cities and main lines of communication and part of the plains. Thus there are extensive areas in the territory under his occupation which he has had to leave ungarrisoned, and which provide a vast arena for our guerrilla warfare. Taking China as a whole, even if the enemy manages to occupy the line connecting Canton, Wuhan and Lanchow and its adjacent areas, he can hardly seize the regions beyond, and this gives China a general rear and vital bases from which to carry on the protracted war to final victory. Secondly, in pitting his small forces against large forces, the enemy is encircled by our large forces. The enemy is attacking us along several routes, strategically he is on exterior lines while we are on interior lines, strategically he is on the offensive while we are on the defensive; all this looks very much to our disadvantage. However, we can make use of our two advantages, namely, our vast territory and large forces, and, instead of stubborn positional warfare, carry on flexible mobile warfare, employing several divisions against one enemy division, several tens of thousands of our men against ten thousand of his, several columns against one of his columns, and suddenly encircling and attacking a single column from the exterior lines of the battlefield. In this way, while the enemy is on exterior lines and on the offensive in strategic operations, he will be forced to fight on interior lines and on the defensive in campaigns and battles. And for us, interior lines and the defensive in strategic operations will be transformed into exterior lines and the offensive in campaigns and battles. This is the way to deal with

one or indeed with any advancing enemy column. Both the consequences discussed above follow from the fact that the enemy is small while we are big. Moreover, the enemy forces, though small, are strong (in arms and in training) while our forces, though large, are weak (in arms and in training but not in morale), and in campaigns and battles, therefore, we should not only employ large forces against small and operate from exterior against interior lines, but also follow the policy of seeking quick decisions. In general, to achieve quick decision, we should attack a moving and not a stationary enemy. We should concentrate a big force under cover beforehand alongside the route which the enemy is sure to take, and while he is on the move, advance suddenly to encircle and attack him before he knows what is happening, and thus quickly conclude the battle. If we fight well, we may destroy the entire enemy force or the greater part or some part of it, and even if we do not fight so well, we may still inflict heavy casualties. This applies to any and every one of our battles. If each month we could win one sizable victory like that at Pinghsingkuan or Taierhchuang, not to speak of more, it would greatly demoralize the enemy, stimulate the morale of our own forces and evoke international support. Thus our strategically protracted war is translated in the held into battles of quick decision. The enemy's war of strategic quick decision is bound to change into protracted war after he is defeated in many campaigns and battles.

75. In a word, the above operational principle for fighting campaigns and battles is one of "quick-decision offensive warfare on exterior lines". It is the opposite of our strategic principle of "protracted defensive warfare on interior lines", and yet it is the indispensable principle for carrying out this strategy. If we should use "protracted defensive warfare on interior lines" as the principle for campaigns and battles too, as we did at the beginning of the War of Resistance, it would be

totally unsuited to the circumstances in which the enemy is small while we are big and the enemy is strong while we are weak; in that case we could never achieve our strategic objective of a protracted war and we would be defeated by the enemy. That is why we have always advocated the organization of the forces of the entire country into a number of large field armies, each counterposed to one of the enemy's field armies but having two, three or four times its strength, and so keeping the enemy engaged in extensive theatres of war in accordance with the principle outlined above. This principle of "quick-decision offensive warfare on exterior lines" can and must be applied in guerrilla as well as in regular warfare. It is applicable not only to any one stage of the war but to its entire course. In the stage of strategic counter-offensive, when we are better equipped technically and are no longer in the position of the weak fighting the strong, we shall be able to capture prisoners and booty on a large scale all the more effectively if we continue to employ superior numbers in quick-decision offensive battles from exterior lines. For instance, if we employ two, three or four mechanized divisions against one mechanized enemy division, we can be all the more certain of destroying it. It is common sense that several hefty fellows can easily beat one.

76. If we resolutely apply "quick-decision offensive warfare on exterior lines" on a battlefield, we shall not only change the balance of forces on that battlefield, but also gradually change the general situation. On the battlefield we shall be on the offensive and the enemy on the defensive, we shall be employing superior numbers on exterior lines and the enemy inferior numbers on interior lines, and we shall seek quick decisions, while the enemy, try as he may, will not be able to protract the fighting in the expectation of reinforcements; for all these reasons, the enemy's position will change from strong to weak, from superior to inferior, while that of our forces will

change from weak to strong, from inferior to superior. After many such battles have been victoriously fought, the general situation between us and the enemy will change. That is to say, through the accumulation of victories on many battlefields by quick-decision offensive warfare on exterior lines, we shall gradually strengthen ourselves and weaken the enemy, which will necessarily affect the general balance of forces and bring about changes in it. When that happens, these changes, together with other factors on our side and together with the changes inside the enemy camp and a favorable international situation, will turn the over-all situation between us and the enemy first into one of parity and then into one of superiority for us. That will be the time for us to launch the counter-offensive and drive the enemy out of the country.

77. War is a contest of strength, but the original pattern of strength changes in the course of war. Here the decisive factor is subjective effort -- winning more victories and committing fewer errors. The objective factors provide the possibility for such change, but in order to turn this possibility into actuality both correct policy and subjective effort are essential. It is then that the subjective plays the decisive role.

# INITIATIVE, FLEXIBILITY AND PLANNING

78. In quick-decision offensive campaigns and battles on exterior lines, as discussed above, the crucial point is the "offensive"; "exterior lines" refers to the sphere of the offensive and "quick-decision" to its duration. Hence the name "quick-decision offensive warfare on exterior lines". It is the best principle for waging a protracted war and it is also the principle for what is known as mobile warfare. But it cannot be put into effect without initiative, flexibility and planning. Let us now study these three questions.

79. We have already discussed man's conscious dynamic role, so why do we talk about the initiative again? By conscious dynamic role we mean conscious action and effort, a characteristic distinguishing man from other beings, and this human characteristic manifests itself most strongly in war; all this has been discussed already. The initiative here means an army's freedom of action as distinguished from an enforced loss of freedom. Freedom of action is the very life of an army and, once it is lost, the army is close to defeat or destruction. The disarming of a soldier is the result of his losing freedom of action through being forced into a passive position. The same is true of the defeat of an army. For this reason both sides in war do all they can to gain the initiative and avoid passivity. It may be said that the quick-decision offensive warfare on exterior lines which we advocate and the flexibility and planning necessary for its execution are designed to gain the initiative and thus force the enemy into a passive position and achieve the object of preserving ourselves and destroying the enemy. But initiative or passivity is inseparable from superiority or inferiority in the capacity to wage war. Consequently it is also inseparable from the correctness or

incorrectness of the subjective direction of war. In addition, there is the question of exploiting the enemy's misconceptions and unpreparedness in order to gain the initiative and force the enemy into passivity. These points are analyzed below.

80. Initiative is inseparable from superiority in capacity to wage war, while passivity is inseparable from inferiority in capacity to wage war. Such superiority or inferiority is the objective basis of initiative or passivity. It is natural that the strategic initiative can be better maintained and exercised through a strategic offensive, but to maintain the initiative always and everywhere, that is, to have the absolute initiative, is possible only when there is absolute superiority matched against absolute inferiority. When a strong, healthy man wrestles with an invalid, he has the absolute initiative. If Japan were not riddled with insoluble contradictions, if, for instance, she could throw in a huge force of several million or ten million men all at once, if her financial resources were several times what they are, if she had no opposition from her own people or from other countries, and if she did not pursue the barbarous policies which arouse the desperate resistance of the Chinese people, then she would be able to maintain absolute superiority and have the absolute initiative always and everywhere. In history, such absolute superiority rarely appears in the early stages of a war or a campaign but is to be found towards its end. For instance, on the eve of Germany's capitulation in World War I, the Entente countries became absolutely superior and Germany absolutely inferior, so that Germany was defeated and the Entente countries were victorious; this is an example of absolute superiority and inferiority towards the end of a war. Again, on the eve of the Chinese victory at Taierhchuang, the isolated Japanese forces there were reduced after bitter fighting to absolute inferiority while our forces achieved absolute superiority, so that the enemy was defeated and we were victorious; this is an example

of absolute superiority and inferiority towards the end of a campaign. A war or campaign may also end in a situation of relative superiority or of parity, in which case there is compromise in the war or stalemate in the campaign. But in most cases it is absolute superiority and inferiority that decide victory and defeat. All this holds for the end of a war or a campaign, and not for the beginning. The outcome of the Sino-Japanese war, it can be predicted, will be that Japan will become absolutely inferior and be defeated and that China will become absolutely superior and gain victory. But at present superiority or inferiority is not absolute on either side, but is relative. With the advantages of her military, economic and political-organizational power, Japan enjoys superiority over us with our military, economic and political-organizational weakness, which creates the basis for her initiative. But since quantitatively her military and other power is not great and she has many other disadvantages, her superiority is reduced by her own contradictions. Upon her invasion of China, her superiority has been reduced still further because she has come up against our vast territory, large population, great numbers of troops and resolute nation-wide resistance. Hence, Japan's general position has become one of only relative superiority, and her ability to exercise and maintain the initiative, which is thereby restricted, has likewise become relative. As for China, though placed in a somewhat passive position strategically because of her inferior strength, she is nevertheless quantitatively superior in territory, population and troops, and also superior in the morale of her people and army and their patriotic hatred of the enemy; this superiority, together with other advantages, reduces the extent of her inferiority in military, economic and other power, and changes it into a relative strategic inferiority. This also reduces the degree of China's passivity so that her strategic position is one of only relative passivity. Any passivity, however, is a disadvantage, and one must strive hard to shake it off. Militarily, the way to do so is resolutely to wage quick-decision offensive warfare on exterior lines, to launch guerrilla warfare in the rear of the enemy and so secure overwhelming local superiority and initiative in many campaigns of mobile and guerrilla warfare. Through such local superiority and local initiative in many campaigns, we can gradually create strategic superiority and strategic initiative and extricate ourselves from strategic inferiority and passivity. Such is the interrelation between initiative and passivity, between superiority and inferiority.

81. From this we can also understand the relationship between initiative or passivity and the subjective directing of war. As already explained, it is possible to escape from our position of relative strategic inferiority and passivity, and the method is to create local superiority and initiative in many campaigns, so depriving the enemy of local superiority and initiative and plunging him into inferiority and passivity. These local successes will add up to strategic superiority and initiative for us and strategic inferiority and passivity for the enemy. Such a change depends upon correct subjective direction. Why? Because while we seek superiority and the initiative, so does the enemy; viewed from this angle, war is a contest in subjective ability between the commanders of the opposing armies in their struggle for superiority and for the initiative on the basis of material conditions such as military forces and financial resources. Out of the contest there emerge a victor and a vanquished; leaving aside the contrast in objective material conditions, the victor will necessarily owe his success to correct subjective direction and the vanquished his defeat to wrong subjective direction. We admit that the phenomenon of war is more elusive and is characterized by greater uncertainty than any other social phenomenon, in other words, that it is more a matter of "probability". Yet war is in no way supernatural, but a mundane process governed by necessity. That is why Sun Wu Tzu's axiom, "Know the enemy

and know yourself, and you can fight a hundred battles with no danger of defeat",[20] remains a scientific truth. Mistakes arise from ignorance about the enemy and about ourselves, and moreover the peculiar nature of war makes it impossible in many cases to have full knowledge about both sides; hence the uncertainty about military conditions and operations, and hence mistakes and defeats. But whatever the situation and the moves in a war, one can know their general aspects and essential points. It is possible for a commander to reduce errors and give generally correct direction, first through all kinds of reconnaissance and then through intelligent inference and judgment. Armed with the weapon of "generally correct direction", we can win more battles and transform our inferiority into superiority and our passivity into initiative. This is how initiative or passivity is related to the correct or incorrect subjective direction of a war.

82. The thesis that incorrect subjective direction can change superiority and initiative into inferiority and passivity, and that correct subjective direction can effect a reverse change, becomes all the more convincing when we look at the record of defeats suffered by big and powerful armies and of victories won by small and weak armies. There are many such instances in Chinese and foreign history. Examples in China are the Battle of Chengpu between the states of Tsin and Chu,[21] the Battle of Chengkao between the states of Chu and Han,[22] the Battle in which Han Hsin defeated the Chao armies,[23] the Battle of Kunyang between the states of Hsin and Han,[24] the Battle of Kuantu between Yuan Shao and Tsao Tsao,[25] the Battle of Chihpi between the states of Wu and Wei,[26] the Battle of Yiling between the states of Wu and Shu,[27] the Battle of Feishui between the states of Chin and Tsin,[28] etc. Among examples to be found abroad are most of Napoleon's campaigns and the civil war in the Soviet Union after the October Revolution. In all these instances, victory was won by

small forces over big and by inferior over superior forces. In every case, the weaker force, pitting local superiority and initiative against the enemy's local inferiority and passivity, first inflicted one sharp defeat on the enemy and then turned on the rest of his forces and smashed them one by one, thus transforming the over-all situation into one of superiority and initiative. The reverse was the case with the enemy who originally had superiority and held the initiative; owing to subjective errors and internal contradictions, it sometimes happened that he completely lost an excellent or fairly good position in which he enjoyed superiority and initiative, and became a general without an army or a king without a kingdom. Thus it can be seen that although superiority or inferiority in the capacity to wage war is the objective basis determining initiative or passivity, it is not in itself actual initiative or passivity; it is only through a struggle, a contest of ability, that actual initiative or passivity can emerge. In the struggle, correct subjective direction can transform inferiority into superiority and passivity into initiative, and incorrect subjective direction can do the opposite. The fact that every ruling dynasty was defeated by revolutionary armies shows that mere superiority in certain respects does not guarantee the initiative, much less the final victory. The inferior side can wrest the initiative and victory from the superior side by securing certain conditions through active subjective endeavor in accordance with the actual circumstances.

83. To have misconceptions and to be caught unawares may mean to lose superiority and initiative. Hence, deliberately creating misconceptions for the enemy and then springing surprise attacks upon him are two ways -- indeed two important means -- of achieving superiority and seizing the initiative. What are misconceptions? "To see every bush and tree on Mount Pakung as an enemy soldier"[29] is an example of

misconception. And "making a feint to the east but attacking in the west" is a way of creating misconceptions among the enemy. When the mass support is sufficiently good to block the leakage of news, it is often possible by various ruses to succeed in leading the enemy into a morass of wrong judgments and actions so that he loses his superiority and the initiative. The saying, "There can never be too much deception in war", means precisely this. What does "being caught unawares" mean? It means being unprepared. Without preparedness superiority is not real superiority and there can be no initiative either. Having grasped this point, a force which is inferior but prepared can often defeat a superior enemy by surprise attack We say an enemy on the move is easy to attack precisely because he is then off guard, that is, unprepared. These two points -- creating misconceptions among the enemy and springing surprise attacks on him -- mean transferring the uncertainties of war to the enemy while securing the greatest possible certainty for ourselves and thereby gaining superiority, the initiative and victory. Excellent organization of the masses is the prerequisite for attaining all this. Therefore it is extremely important to arouse all the people who are opposed to the enemy, to arm themselves to the last man, make widespread raids on the enemy and also prevent the leakage of news and provide a screen for our own forces; in this way the enemy will be kept in the dark about where and when our forces will attack, and an objective basis will be created for misconceptions and unpreparedness on his part. It was largely owing to the organized, armed masses of the people that the weak and small force of the Chinese Red Army was able to win many battles in the period of the Agrarian Revolutionary War. Logically, a national war should win broader mass support than an agrarian revolutionary war; however, as a result of past mistakes [30] the people are in an unorganized state, cannot be promptly drawn in to serve the cause and are sometimes even made use of by the enemy. The resolute rallying of the people on a broad scale is the only way to secure inexhaustible resources to meet all the requirements of the war. Moreover, it will definitely play a big part in carrying out our tactics of defeating the enemy by misleading him and catching him unawares. We are not Duke Hsiang of Sung and have no use for his asinine ethics.[31] In order to achieve victory we must as far as possible make the enemy blind and deaf by sealing his eyes and ears and drive his commanders to distraction by creating confusion in their minds. The above concerns the way in which the initiative or passivity is related to the subjective direction of the war. Such subjective direction is indispensable for defeating Japan.

84. By and large, Japan has held the initiative in the stage of her offensive by reason of her military power and her exploitation of our subjective errors, past and present. But her initiative is beginning to wane to some extent because of her many inherent disadvantages and of the subjective errors she too has committed in the course of the war (of which more later) and also because of our many advantages. The enemy's defeat at Taierhchuang and his predicament in Shansi prove this clearly. The widespread development of guerrilla warfare in the enemy's rear has placed his garrisons in the occupied areas in a completely passive position. Although he is still on the offensive strategically and still holds the initiative, his initiative will end when his strategic offensive ends. The first reason why the enemy will not be able to maintain the initiative is that his shortage of troops renders it impossible for him to carry on the offensive indefinitely. Our offensive warfare in campaigns and our guerrilla warfare behind the enemy lines, together with other factors, constitute the second reason why he will have to cease his offensive at a certain limit and will not be able to keep his initiative. The existence of the Soviet Union and changes in the international situation constitute the third reason. Thus it can be seen that the enemy's initiative is limited

and can be shattered. If, in military operations, China can keep up offensive warfare by her main forces in campaigns and battles, vigorously develop guerrilla warfare in the enemy's rear and mobilize the people on a broad scale politically, we can gradually build up a position of strategic initiative.

85. Let us now discuss flexibility. What is flexibility? It is the concrete realization of the initiative in military operations; it is the flexible employment of armed forces. The flexible employment of armed forces is the central task in directing a war, a task most difficult to perform well. In addition to organizing and educating the army and the people, the business of war consists in the employment of troops in combat, and all these things are done to win the fight. Of course it is difficult to organize an army, etc., but it is even more difficult to employ it, particularly when the weak are fighting the strong. To do so requires subjective ability of a very high order and requires the overcoming of the confusion, obscurity and uncertainty peculiar to war and the discovery of order, clarity and certainty in it; only thus can flexibility in command be realized.

86. The basic principle of field operations for the War of Resistance against Japan is quick-decision offensive warfare on exterior lines. There are various tactics or methods for giving effect to this principle, such as dispersion and concentration of forces, diverging advance and converging attack, the offensive and the defensive, assault and containment, encirclement and outflanking, advance and retreat. It is easy to understand these tactics, but not at all easy to employ and vary them flexibly. Here the three crucial links are the time, the place and the troops. No victory can be won unless the time, the place and the troops are well chosen. For example, in attacking an enemy force on the move, if we strike too early, we expose ourselves and give the enemy a chance to prepare, and if we strike too late, the enemy may have encamped and concentrated his

forces, presenting us with a hard nut to crack. This is the question of the time. If we select a point of assault on the left flank which actually turns out to be the enemy's weak point, victory will be easy; but if we select the right flank and hit a snag, nothing will be achieved. This is the question of the place. If a particular unit of our forces is employed for a particular task, victory may be easy; but if another unit is employed for the same task, it may be hard to achieve results. This is the question of the troops. We should know not only how to employ tactics but how to vary them. For flexibility of command the important task is to make changes such as from the offensive to the defensive or from the defensive to the offensive, from advance to retreat or from retreat to advance, from containment to assault or from assault to containment, from encirclement to outflanking or from outflanking to encirclement, and to make such changes properly and in good time according to the circumstances of the troops and terrain on both sides. This is true of command in campaigns and strategic command as well as of command in battles.

87. The ancients said: "Ingenuity in varying tactics depends on mother wit"; this "ingenuity", which is what we mean by flexibility, is the contribution of the intelligent commander. Flexibility does not mean recklessness; recklessness must be rejected. Flexibility consists in the intelligent commander's ability to take timely and appropriate measures on the basis of objective conditions after "judging the hour and sizing up the situation" (the "situation" includes the enemy's situation, our situation and the terrain), and this flexibility is "ingenuity in varying tactics". On the basis of this ingenuity, we can win more victories in quick-decision offensive warfare on exterior lines, change the balance of forces in our favor, gain the initiative over the enemy, and overwhelm and crush him so that the final victory will be ours.

88. Let us now discuss the question of planning. Because of the uncertainty peculiar to war, it is much more difficult to prosecute war according to plan than is the case with other activities. Yet, since "preparedness ensures success and unpreparedness spells failure", there can be no victory in war without advance planning and preparations. There is no absolute certainty in war, and yet it is not without some degree of relative certainty. We are comparatively certain about our own situation. We are very uncertain about the enemy's, but here too there are signs for us to read, clues to follow and sequences of phenomena to ponder. These form what we call a degree of relative certainty, which provides an objective basis for planning in war. Modern technical developments (telegraphy, radio, aeroplanes, motor vehicles, railways, steamships, etc.) have added to the possibilities of planning in war. However, complete or stable planning is difficult because there is only very limited and transient certainty in war; such planning must change with the movement (flow or change) of the war and vary in degree according to the scale of the war. Tactical plans, such as plans for attack or defense by small formations or units, often have to be changed several times a day. A plan of campaign, that is, of action by large formations, can generally stand till the conclusion of the campaign, in the course of which, however, it is often changed partially or sometimes even wholly. A strategic plan based on the over-all situation of both belligerents is still more stable, but it too is applicable only in a given strategic stage and has to be changed when the war moves towards a new stage. The making and changing of tactical, campaign and strategic plans in accordance with scope and circumstance is a key factor in directing a war; it is the concrete expression of flexibility in war, in other words, it is also ingenuity in varying one's tactics. Commanders at all levels in the anti-Japanese war should take note.

89. Because of the fluidity of war, some people categorically deny that war plans or policies can be relatively stable, describing such plans or policies as "mechanical". This view is wrong. In the preceding section we fully recognized that, because the circumstances of war are only relatively certain and the flow (movement or change) of war is rapid, war plans or policies can be only relatively stable and have to be changed or revised in good time in accordance with changing circumstances and the flow of the war; otherwise we would become mechanists. But one must not deny the need for war plans or policies that are relatively stable over given periods; to negate this is to negate everything, including the war itself as well as the negator himself. As both military conditions and operations are relatively stable, we must grant the relative stability of the war plans and policies resulting from them. For example, since both the circumstances of the war in northern China and the dispersed nature of the Eighth Route Army's operations are relatively stable for a particular stage, it is absolutely necessary during this stage to acknowledge the relative stability of the Eighth Route Army's strategic principle of operation, namely, "Guerrilla warfare is basic, but lose no chance for mobile warfare under favorable conditions." The period of validity of a plan for a campaign is shorter than that of a strategic plan, and for a tactical plan it is shorter still, but each is stable over a given period. Anyone denying this point would have no way of handling warfare and would become a relativist in war with no settled views, for whom one course is just as wrong or just as right as another. No one denies that even a plan valid for a given period is fluid; otherwise, one plan would never be abandoned in favor of another. But it is fluid within limits, fluid within the bounds of the various war operations undertaken for carrying it out, but not fluid as to its essence; in other words, it is quantitatively but not qualitatively fluid. Within such a given period of time, this essence is definitely not fluid, which is what we mean by relative stability

within a given period. In the great river of absolute fluidity throughout the war there is relative stability at each particular stretch -- such is our fundamental view regarding war plans or policies.

90. Having dealt with protracted defensive warfare on interior lines in strategy and with quick-decision offensive warfare on exterior lines in campaigns and battles, and also with the initiative, flexibility and planning, we can now sum up briefly. The anti-Japanese war must have a plan. War plans, which are the concrete application of strategy and tactics, must be flexible so that they can be adapted to the circumstances of the war. We should always seek to transform our inferiority into superiority and our passivity into the initiative so as to change the situation as between the enemy and ourselves. All these find expression in quick-decision offensive warfare on exterior lines in campaigns and battles and protracted defensive warfare on interior lines in strategy.

# MOBILE WARFARE, GUERRILLA WARFARE AND POSITIONAL WARFARE

91. A war will take the form of mobile warfare when its content is quick-decision offensive warfare on exterior lines in campaigns and battles within the framework of the strategy of interior lines, protracted war and defense. Mobile warfare is the form in which regular armies wage quick-decision offensive campaigns and battles on exterior lines along extensive fronts and over big areas of operation. At the same time, it includes "mobile defense", which is conducted when necessary to facilitate such offensive battles; it also includes positional attack and positional defense in a supplementary role. Its characteristics are regular armies, superiority of forces in campaigns and battles, the offensive, and fluidity.

92. China has a vast territory and an immense number of soldiers, but her troops are inadequately equipped and trained; the enemy's forces, on the other hand, are inadequate in number, but better equipped and trained. In this situation, there is no doubt that we must adopt offensive mobile warfare as our primary form of warfare, supplementing it by others and integrating them all into mobile warfare. We must oppose "only retreat, never advance", which is flightism, and at the same time oppose "only advance, never retreat", which is desperate recklessness.

93. One of the characteristics of mobile warfare is fluidity, which not only permits but requires a field army to advance and to withdraw in great strides. However, it has nothing in common with flightism of the Han Fu-chu brand.[32] The primary requirement of war is to destroy the enemy, and the other requirement is self-preservation. The object of self-preservation is to destroy the enemy, and to destroy the enemy

is in turn the most effective means of self-preservation. Hence mobile warfare is in no way an excuse for people like Han Fu-chu and can never mean moving only backward, and never forward; that kind of "moving" which negates the basic offensive character of mobile warfare would, in practice, "move" China out of existence despite her vastness.

94. However, the other view, which we call the desperate recklessness of "only advance, never retreat", is also wrong. The mobile warfare we advocate, the content of which is quick-decision offensive warfare on exterior lines in campaigns and battles, includes positional warfare in a supplementary role, "mobile defense" and retreat, without all of which mobile warfare cannot be fully carried out. Desperate recklessness is military short-sightedness, originating often from fear of losing territory. A man who acts with desperate recklessness does not know that one characteristic of mobile warfare is fluidity, which not only permits but requires a field army to advance and to withdraw in great strides. On the positive side, in order to draw the enemy into a fight unfavorable to him but favorable to us, it is usually necessary that he should be on the move and that we should have a number of advantages, such as favorable terrain, a vulnerable enemy, a local population that can prevent the leakage of information, and the enemy's fatigue and unpreparedness. This requires that the enemy should advance, and we should not grudge a temporary loss of part of our territory. For the temporary loss of part of our territory is the price we pay for the permanent preservation of all our territory, including the recovery of lost territory. On the negative side, whenever we are forced into a disadvantageous position which fundamentally endangers the preservation of our forces, we should have the courage to retreat, so as to preserve our forces and hit the enemy when new opportunities arise. In their ignorance of this principle, the advocates of desperate action will contest a city or a piece of ground even when the position

is obviously and definitely unfavorable; as a result, they not only lose the city or ground but fail to preserve their forces. We have always advocated the policy of "luring the enemy in deep", precisely because it is the most effective military policy for a weak army strategically on the defensive to employ against a strong army.

95. Among the forms of warfare in the anti-Japanese war mobile warfare comes first and guerrilla warfare second. When we say that in the entire war mobile warfare is primary and guerrilla warfare supplementary, we mean that the outcome of the war depends mainly on regular warfare, especially in its mobile form, and that guerrilla warfare cannot shoulder the main responsibility in deciding the outcome. It does not follow, however, that the role of guerrilla warfare is unimportant in the strategy of the war. Its role in the strategy of the war as a whole is second only to that of mobile warfare, for without its support we cannot defeat the enemy. In saying this we also have in mind the strategic task of developing guerrilla warfare into mobile warfare. Guerrilla warfare will not remain the same throughout this long and cruel war, but will rise to a higher level and develop into mobile warfare. Thus the strategic role of guerrilla warfare is twofold, to support regular warfare and to transform itself into regular warfare. Considering the unprecedented extent and duration of guerrilla warfare in China's War of Resistance, it is all the more important not to underestimate its strategic role. Guerrilla warfare in China, therefore, has not only its tactical but also its peculiar strategic problems. I have already discussed this in "Problems of Strategy in Guerrilla War against Japan". As indicated above, the forms of warfare in the three strategic stages of the War of Resistance are as follows. In the first stage mobile warfare is primary, while guerrilla and positional warfare are supplementary. In the second stage guerrilla warfare will advance to the first place and will be supplemented by mobile

and positional warfare. In the third stage mobile warfare will again become the primary form and will be supplemented by positional and guerrilla warfare. But the mobile warfare of the third stage will no longer be undertaken solely by the original regular forces; part, possibly quite an important part, will be undertaken by forces which were originally guerrillas but which will have progressed from guerrilla to mobile warfare. From the view point of all three stages in China's War of Resistance against Japan, guerrilla warfare is definitely indispensable. Our guerrilla war will present a great drama unparalleled in the annals of war. For this reason, out of the millions of China's regular troops, it is absolutely necessary to assign at least several hundred thousand to disperse through all enemy-occupied areas, arouse the masses to arm themselves, and wage guerrilla warfare in co-ordination with the masses. The regular forces so assigned should shoulder this sacred task conscientiously, and they should not think their status lowered because they fight fewer big battles and for the time being do not appear as national heroes. Any such thinking is wrong. Guerrilla warfare does not bring as quick results or as great renown as regular warfare, but "a long road tests a horse's strength and a long task proves a man's heart", and in the course of this long and cruel war guerrilla warfare will demonstrate its immense power; it is indeed no ordinary under taking. Moreover, such regular forces can conduct guerrilla warfare when dispersed and mobile warfare when concentrated, as the Eighth Route Army has been doing. The principle of the Eighth Route Army is, "Guerrilla warfare is basic, but lose no chance for mobile warfare under favorable conditions." This principle is perfectly correct; the views of its opponents are wrong.

96. At China's present technical level, positional warfare, defensive or offensive, is generally impracticable, and this is where our weakness manifests itself. Moreover, the enemy is

also exploiting the vastness of our territory to bypass our fortified positions. Hence positional warfare cannot be an important, still less the principal, means for us. But in the first and second stages of the war, it is possible and essential, within the scope of mobile warfare, to employ localized positional warfare in a supplementary role in campaigns. Semi-positional "mobile defense" is a still more essential part of mobile warfare undertaken for the purpose of resisting the enemy at every step, thereby depleting his forces and gaining extra time. China must strive to increase her supplies of modern weapons so that she can fully carry out the tasks of positional attack in the stage of the strategic counter-offensive. In this third stage positional warfare will undoubtedly play a greater role, for then the enemy will be holding fast to his positions, and we shall not be able to recover our lost territory unless we launch powerful positional attacks in support of mobile warfare. Nevertheless, in the third stage too, we must exert our every effort to make mobile warfare the primary form of warfare. For the art of directing war and the active role of man are largely nullified in positional warfare such as that fought in Western Europe in the second half of World War I. It is only natural that the war should be taken "out of the trenches", since the war is being fought in the vast expanses of China and since our side will remain poorly equipped technically for quite a long time. Even during the third stage, when China's technical position will be better, she will hardly surpass her enemy in that respect, and so will have to concentrate on highly mobile warfare, without which she cannot achieve final victory. Hence, throughout the War of Resistance China will not adopt positional warfare as primary; the primary or important forms are mobile warfare and guerrilla warfare. These two forms of warfare will afford full play to the art of directing war and to the active role of man -- what a piece of good fortune out of our misfortune!

# WAR OF ATTRITION AND WAR OF ANNIHILATION

97. As we have said before, the essence, or the object, of war is to preserve oneself and destroy the enemy. Since there are three forms of warfare, mobile, positional and guerrilla, for achieving this object, and since they differ in degrees of effectiveness, there arises the broad distinction between war of attrition and war of annihilation.

98. To begin with, we may say that the anti-Japanese war is at once a war of attrition and a war of annihilation. Why? Because the enemy is still exploiting his strength and retains strategic superiority and strategic initiative, and therefore, unless we fight campaigns and battles of annihilation, we cannot effectively and speedily reduce his strength and break his superiority and initiative. We still have our weakness and have not yet rid ourselves of strategic inferiority and passivity; therefore, unless we fight campaigns and battles of annihilation, we cannot win time to improve our internal and international situation and alter our unfavorable position. Hence campaigns of annihilation are the means of attaining the objective of strategic attrition. In this sense war of annihilation is war of attrition. It is chiefly by using the method of attrition through annihilation that China can wage protracted war.

99. But the objective of strategic attrition may also be achieved by campaigns of attrition. Generally speaking, mobile warfare performs the task of annihilation, positional warfare performs the task of attrition, and guerrilla warfare performs both simultaneously; the three forms of warfare are thus distinguished from one another. In this sense war of annihilation is different from war of attrition. Campaigns of attrition are supplementary but necessary in protracted war.

100. Speaking theoretically and in terms of China's needs, in order to achieve the strategic objective of greatly depleting the enemy's forces, China in her defensive stage should not only exploit the function of annihilation, which is fulfilled primarily by mobile warfare and partially by guerrilla warfare, but also exploit the function of attrition, which is fulfilled primarily by positional warfare (which itself is supplementary) and partially by guerrilla warfare. In the stage of stalemate we should continue to exploit the functions of annihilation and attrition fulfilled by guerrilla and mobile warfare for further large-scale depletion of the enemy's forces. All this is aimed at protracting the war, gradually changing the general balance of forces and preparing the conditions for our counter-offensive. During the strategic counter-offensive, we should continue to employ the method of attrition through annihilation so as finally to expel the enemy.

101. But as a matter of fact, it was our experience in the last ten months that many or even most of the mobile warfare campaigns became campaigns of attrition, and guerrilla warfare did not adequately fulfill its proper function of annihilation in certain areas. The positive aspect is that at least we depleted the enemy's forces, which is important both for the protracted warfare and for our final victory, and did not shed our blood in vain. But the drawbacks are first, that we did not sufficiently deplete the enemy, and second, that we were unable to avoid rather heavy losses and captured little war booty. Although we should recognize the objective cause of this situation, namely, the disparity between us and the enemy in technical equipment and in the training of troops, in any case it is necessary, both theoretically and practically, to urge that our main forces should fight vigorous battles of annihilation whenever circumstances are favorable. And although our guerrilla units have to wage battles of pure attrition in performing specific

tasks such as sabotage and harassment, it is necessary to advocate and vigorously carry out campaigns and battles of annihilation whenever circumstances are favorable, so as greatly to deplete the enemy's forces and greatly replenish our own.

102. The "exterior lines", the "quick-decision" and the "offensive" in quick-decision offensive warfare on exterior lines and the "mobility" in mobile warfare find their main operational expression in the use of encircling and outflanking tactics; hence the necessity for concentrating superior forces. Therefore concentration of forces and the use of encircling and outflanking tactics are the prerequisites for mobile warfare, that is, for quick-decision offensive warfare on exterior lines. All this is aimed at annihilating the enemy forces.

103. The strength of the Japanese army lies not only in its weapons but also in the training of its officers and men -- its degree of organization, its self-confidence arising from never having been defeated, its superstitious belief in the Mikado and in supernatural beings, its arrogance, its contempt for the Chinese people and other such characteristics, all of which stem from long years of indoctrination by the Japanese warlords and from the Japanese national tradition. This is the chief reason why we have taken very few prisoners, although we have killed and wounded a great many enemy troops. It is a point that has been underestimated by many people in the past. To destroy these enemy characteristics will be a long process. The first thing to do is to give the matter serious attention, and then patiently and systematically to work at it in the political field and in the fields of international propaganda and the Japanese people's movement; in the military sphere war of annihilation is of course one of the means. In these enemy characteristics pessimists may and a basis for the theory of national subjugation, and passively minded military men a

basis for opposition to war of annihilation. We, on the contrary, maintain that these strong points of the Japanese army can be destroyed and that their destruction has already begun. The chief method of destroying them is to win over the Japanese soldiers politically. We should understand, rather than hurt, their pride and channel it in the proper direction and, by treating prisoners of war leniently, lead the Japanese soldiers to see the anti-popular character of the aggression committed by the Japanese rulers. On the other hand, we should demonstrate to the Japanese soldiers the indomitable spirit and the heroic, stubborn fighting capacity of the Chinese army and the Chinese people, that is, we should deal them blows in battles of annihilation. Our experience in the last ten months of military operations shows that it is possible to annihilate enemy forces -- witness the Pinghsingkuan and Taierhchuang campaigns. The Japanese army's morale is beginning to sag, its soldiers do not understand the aim of the war, they are engulfed by the Chinese armies and by the Chinese people, in assault they show far less courage than the Chinese soldiers, and so on; all these are objective factors favorable to waging battles of annihilation, and they will, moreover, steadily develop as the war becomes protracted. From the viewpoint of destroying the enemy's overweening arrogance through battles of annihilation, such battles are one of the prerequisites for shortening the war and accelerating the emancipation of the Japanese soldiers and the Japanese people. Cats make friends with cats, and nowhere in the world do cats make friends with mice.

104. On the other hand, it must be admitted that for the present we are inferior to the enemy in technical equipment and in troop training. Therefore, it is often difficult to achieve the maximum in annihilation, such as capturing the whole or the greater part of an enemy force, especially when fighting on the plains. In this connection the excessive demands of the theorists of quick victory are wrong. What should be demanded

of our forces in the anti-Japanese war is that they should fight battles of annihilation as far as possible. In favorable circumstances, we should concentrate superior forces in every battle and employ encircling and outflanking tactics -- encircle part if not all of the enemy forces, capture part if not all of the encircled forces, and inflict heavy casualties on part of the encircled forces if we cannot capture them. In circumstances which are unfavorable for battles of annihilation, we should fight battles of attrition. In favorable circumstances, we should employ the principle of concentration of forces, and in unfavorable circumstances that of their dispersion. As for the relationship of command in campaigns, we should apply the principle of centralized command in the former and that of decentralized command in the latter. These are the basic principles of field operations for the War of Resistance against Japan.

# THE POSSIBILITIES OF EXPLOITING
# THE ENEMY'S MISTAKES

105. The enemy command itself provides a basis for the possibility of defeating Japan. History has never known an infallible general, and the enemy makes mistakes just as we ourselves can hardly avoid making them; hence, the possibility exists of exploiting the enemy's errors. In the ten months of his war of aggression the enemy has already made many mistakes in strategy and tactics. There are five major ones.

First, piecemeal reinforcement. This is due to the enemy's underestimation of China and also to his shortage of troops. The enemy has always looked down on us. After grabbing the four northeastern provinces at small cost, he occupied eastern Hopei and northern Chahar, all by way of strategic reconnaissance. The conclusion the enemy came to was that the Chinese nation is a heap of loose sand. Thus, thinking that China would crumble at a single blow, he mapped out a plan of "quick decision", attempting with very small forces to send us scampering in panic. He did not expect to find such great unity and such immense powers of resistance as China has shown during the past ten months, forgetting as he did that China is already in an era of progress and already has an advanced political party, an advanced army and an advanced people. Meeting with setbacks, the enemy then increased his forces piecemeal from about a dozen to thirty divisions. If he wants to advance, he will have to augment his forces still further. But because of Japan's antagonism with the Soviet Union and her inherent shortage of manpower and finances, there are inevitable limits to the maximum number of men she can throw in and to the furthest extent of her advance.

Second, absence of a main direction of attack. Before the Taierhchuang campaign, the enemy had divided his forces more or less evenly between northern and central China and had again divided them inside each of these areas. In northern China, for instance, he divided his forces among the Tientsin-Pukow, the Peiping-Hankow and the Tatung-Puchow Railways, and along each of these lines he suffered some casualties and left some garrisons in the places occupied, after which he lacked the forces for further advances. After the Taierhchuang defeat, from which he learned a lesson, the enemy concentrated his main forces in the direction of Hsuchow, and so temporarily corrected this mistake.

Third, lack of strategic co-ordination. On the whole co-ordination exists within the groups of enemy forces in northern China and in central China, but there is glaring lack of co ordination between the two. When his forces on the southern section of the Tientsin-Pukow Railway attacked Hsiaopengpu, those on the northern section made no move, and when his forces on the northern section attacked Taierhchuang, those on the southern section made no move. After the enemy came to grief at both places, the Japanese minister of war arrived on an inspection tour and the chief of general staff turned up to take charge, and for the moment, it seemed, there was co-ordination. The landlord class, the bourgeoisie and the warlords of Japan have very serious internal contradictions, which are growing, and the lack of military co-ordination is one of the concrete manifestations of this fact.

Fourth, failure to grasp strategic opportunities. This failure was conspicuously shown in the enemy's halt after the occupation of Nanking and Taiyuan, chiefly because of his shortage of troops and his lack of a strategic pursuit force.

Fifth, encirclement of large, but annihilation of small, numbers. Before the Taierhchuang campaign, in the campaigns of Shanghai, Nanking, Tsangchow, Paoting, Nankow, Hsinkou and Linfen, many Chinese troops were routed but few were taken prisoner, which shows the stupidity of the enemy command.

These five errors -- piecemeal reinforcement, absence of a main direction of attack, lack of strategic co-ordination, failure to grasp opportunities, and encirclement of large, but annihilation of small, numbers -- were all points of incompetence in the Japanese command before the Taierhchuang campaign. Although the enemy has since made some improvements, he cannot possibly avoid repeating his errors because of his shortage of troops, his internal contradictions and other factors. In addition, what he gains at one point he loses at another. For instance, when he concentrated his forces in northern China on Hsuchow, he left a great vacuum in the occupied areas in northern China, which gave us full scope for developing guerrilla warfare. These mistakes were of the enemy's own making and not induced by us. On our part, we can deliberately make the enemy commit errors, that is, we can mislead him and maneuver him into the desired position by ingenious and effective moves with the help of a well-organized local population, for example, by "making a feint to the east but attacking in the west". This possibility has already been discussed. All the above shows that in the enemy's command, too, we can find some basis for victory. Of course, we should not take it as an important basis for our strategic planning; on the contrary, the only reliable course is to base our planning on the assumption that the enemy will make few mistakes. Besides, the enemy can exploit our mistakes just as we can exploit his. It is the duty of our command to allow him the minimum of opportunities for doing so. Actually, the enemy command has committed errors, will again commit errors in the future, and can be made to do so through our endeavors. All these errors we can exploit, and it is the business of our generals in the War of Resistance to do their utmost to seize upon them. However, although much of the enemy's strategic and campaign command is incompetent, there are quite a few excellent points in his battle command, that is, in his unit and small formation tactics, and here we should learn from him.

*Mao Zedong*

# THE QUESTION OF DECISIVE ENGAGEMENTS
# IN THE ANTI-JAPANESE WAR

106. The question of decisive engagements in the anti-Japanese war should be approached from three aspects: we should resolutely fight a decisive engagement in every campaign or battle in which we are sure of victory; we should avoid a decisive engagement in every campaign or battle in which we are not sure of victory; and we should absolutely avoid a strategically decisive engagement on which the fate of the whole nation is staked. The characteristics differentiating our War of Resistance against Japan from many other wars are also revealed in this question of decisive engagements. In the first and second stages of the war, which are marked by the enemy's strength and our weakness, the enemy's objective is to have us concentrate our main forces for a decisive engagement. Our objective is exactly the opposite. We want to choose conditions favorable to us, concentrate superior forces and fight decisive campaigns or battles only when we are sure of victory, as in the battles at Pinghsingkuan, Taierhchuang and other places; we want to avoid decisive engagements under unfavorable conditions when we are not sure of victory, this being the policy we adopted in the Changteh and other campaigns. As for fighting a strategically decisive engagement on which the fate of the whole nation is staked, we simply must not do so, as witness the recent withdrawal from Hsuchow. The enemy's plan for a "quick decision" was thus foiled, and now he cannot help fighting a protracted war with us. These principles are impracticable in a country with a small territory, and hardly practicable in a country that is very backward politically. They are practicable in China because she is a big country and is in an era of progress. If strategically decisive engagements are avoided, then "as long as the green mountains

are there, one need not worry about firewood", for even though some of our territory may be lost, we shall still have plenty of room for maneuver and thus be able to promote and await domestic progress, international support and the internal disintegration of the enemy; that is the best policy for us in the anti-Japanese war. Unable to endure the arduous trials of a protracted war and eager for an early triumph, the impetuous theorists of quick victory clamor for a strategically decisive engagement the moment the situation takes a slightly favorable turn. To do what they want would be to inflict incalculable damage on the entire war, spell finis to the protracted war, and land us in the enemy's deadly trap; actually, it would be the worst policy. Undoubtedly, if we are to avoid decisive engagements, we shall have to abandon territory, and we must have the courage to do so when (and only when) it becomes completely unavoidable. At such times we should not feel the slightest regret, for this policy of trading space for time is correct. History tells us how Russia made a courageous retreat to avoid a decisive engagement and then defeated Napoleon, the terror of his age. Today China should do likewise.

107. Are we not afraid of being denounced as "non-resisters"? No, we are not. Not to fight at all but to compromise with the enemy -- that is non-resistance, which should not only be denounced but must never be tolerated. We must resolutely fight the War of Resistance, but in order to avoid the enemy's deadly trap, it is absolutely necessary that we should not allow our main forces to be finished off at one blow, which would make it difficult to continue the War of Resistance -- in brief, it is absolutely necessary to avoid national subjugation. To have doubts on this point is to be short sighted on the question of the war and is sure to lead one into the ranks of the subjugationists. We have criticized the desperate recklessness of "only advance, never retreat" precisely because, if it became the fashion, this doctrine would make it impossible to continue the War of

Resistance and would lead to the danger of ultimate national subjugation.

108. We are for decisive engagements whenever circumstances are favorable, whether in battles or in major or minor campaigns, and in this respect we should never tolerate passivity. Only through such decisive engagements can we achieve the objective of annihilating or depleting the enemy forces, and every soldier in the anti-Japanese war should resolutely play his part. For this purpose considerable partial sacrifices are necessary; to avoid any sacrifice whatsoever is the attitude of cowards and of those afflicted by the fear of Japan and must be firmly opposed. The execution of Li Fu-ying, Han Fu-chu and other flightists was justified. Within the scope of correct war planning, encouraging the spirit and practice of heroic self-sacrifice and dauntless advance in battle is absolutely necessary and inseparable from the waging of protracted war and the achievement of final victory. We have strongly condemned the flightism of "only retreat, never advance" and have supported the strict enforcement of discipline, because it is only through heroic decisive engagements, fought under a correct plan, that we can vanquish the powerful enemy; flightism, on the contrary, gives direct support to the theory of national subjugation.

109. Is it not self-contradictory to fight heroically first and then abandon territory? Will not our heroic fighters have shed their blood in vain? That is not at all the way questions should be posed. To eat and then to empty your bowels -- is this not to eat in vain? To sleep and then to get up -- is this not to sleep in vain? Can questions be posed in such a way? I would suppose not. To keep on eating, to keep on sleeping, to keep on fighting heroically all the way to the Yalu River without a stop -- these are subjectivist and formalist illusions, not realities of life. As everybody knows, although in fighting and shedding our blood

in order to gain time and prepare the counter-offensive we have had to abandon some territory, in fact we have gained time, we have achieved the objective of annihilating and depleting enemy forces, we have acquired experience in fighting, we have aroused hitherto inactive people and improved our international standing. Has our blood been shed in vain? Certainly not. Territory has been given up in order to preserve our military forces and indeed to preserve territory, because if we do not abandon part of our territory when conditions are unfavorable but blindly fight decisive engagements without the least assurance of winning, we shall lose our military forces and then be unable to avoid the loss of all our territory, to say nothing of recovering territory already lost. A capitalist must have capital to run his business, and if he loses it all he is no longer a capitalist. Even a gambler must have money to stake, and if he risks it all on a single throw and his luck fails, he cannot gamble any more. Events have their twists and turns and do not follow a straight line, and war is no exception; only formalists are unable to comprehend this truth.

110. I think the same will also hold true for the decisive engagements in the stage of strategic counter-offensive. Although by then the enemy will be in the inferior and we in the superior position, the principle of "fighting profitable decisive engagements and avoiding unprofitable ones" will still apply and will continue to apply until we have fought our way to the Yalu River. This is how we will be able to maintain our initiative from beginning to end, and as for the enemy's "challenges" and other people's "taunts", we should imperturbably brush them aside and ignore them. In the War of Resistance only those generals who show this kind of firmness can be deemed courageous and wise. This is beyond the ken of those who "jump whenever touched". Even though we are in a more or less passive position strategically in this first stage of the war, we should have the initiative in every campaign; and

of course we should have the initiative throughout the later stages. We are for protracted war and final victory; we are not gamblers who risk everything on a single throw.

# THE ARMY AND THE PEOPLE ARE
# THE FOUNDATION OF VICTORY

111. Japanese imperialism will never relax in its aggression against and repression of revolutionary China; this is determined by its imperialist nature. If China did not resist, Japan would easily seize all China without firing a single shot, as she did the four northeastern provinces. Since China is resisting, it is an inexorable law that Japan will try to repress this resistance until the force of her repression is exceeded by the force of China's resistance. The Japanese landlord class and bourgeoisie are very ambitious, and in order to drive south to Southeast Asia and north to Siberia, they have adopted the policy of breaking through in the center by first attacking China. Those who think that Japan will know where to stop and be content with the occupation of northern China and of Kiangsu and Chekiang Provinces completely fail to perceive that imperialist Japan, which has developed to a new stage and is approaching extinction, differs from the Japan of the past. When we say that there is a definite limit both to the number of men Japan can throw in and to the extent of her advance, we mean that with her available strength, Japan can only commit part of her forces against China and only penetrate China as far as their capacity allows, for she also wants to attack in other directions and has to defend herself against other enemies; at the same time China has given proof of progress and capacity for stubborn resistance, and it is inconceivable that there should be fierce attacks by Japan without in evitable resistance by China. Japan cannot occupy the whole of China, but she will spare no effort to suppress China's resistance in all the areas she can reach, and will not stop until internal and external developments push Japanese imperialism to the brink of the grave. There are only two possible outcomes to the political situation in Japan. Either the downfall of her entire ruling class

occurs rapidly, political power passes to the people and war thus comes to an end, which is impossible at the moment; or her landlord class and bourgeoisie become more and more fascist and maintain the war until the day of their downfall, which is the very road Japan is now travelling. There can be no other outcome. Those who hope that the moderates among the Japanese bourgeoisie will come forward and stop the war are only harboring illusions. The reality of Japanese politics for many years has been that the bourgeois moderates of Japan have fallen captive to the landlords and the financial magnates. Now that Japan has launched war against China, so long as she does not suffer a fatal blow from Chinese resistance and still retains sufficient strength, she is bound to attack Southeast Asia or Siberia, or even both. She will do so once war breaks out in Europe; in their wishful calculations, the rulers of Japan have it worked out on a grandiose scale. Of course. it is possible that Japan will have to drop her original plan of invading Siberia and adopt a mainly defensive attitude towards the Soviet Union on account of Soviet strength and of the serious extent to which Japan herself has been weakened by her war against China. But in that case, so far from relaxing her aggression against China she will intensify it, because then the only way left to her will be to gobble up the weak. China's task of persevering in the War of Resistance, the united front and the protracted war will then become all the more weighty, and it will be all the more necessary not to slacken our efforts in the slightest.

112. Under the circumstances the main prerequisites for China's victory over Japan are nation-wide unity and all-round progress on a scale ten or even a hundred times greater than in the past. China is already in an era of progress and has achieved a splendid unity, but her progress and unity are still far from adequate. That Japan has occupied such an extensive area is due not only to her strength but also to China's

weakness; this weakness is entirely the cumulative effect of the various historical errors of the last hundred years, and especially of the last ten years, which have confined progress to its present bounds. It is impossible to vanquish so strong an enemy without making an extensive and long-term effort. There are many things we have to exert ourselves to do; here I will deal only with two fundamental aspects, the progress of the army and the progress of the people.

113. The reform of our military system requires its modernization and improved technical equipment, without which we cannot drive the enemy back across the Yalu River. In our employment of troops we need progressive, flexible strategy and tactics, without which we likewise cannot win victory. Nevertheless, soldiers are the foundation of an arrny; unless they are imbued with a progressive political spirit, and unless such a spirit is fostered through progressive political work, it will be impossible to achieve genuine unity between officers and men, impossible to arouse their enthusiasm for the War of Resistance to the full, and impossible to provide a sound basis for the most effective use of all our technical equipment and tactics. When we say that Japan will finally be defeated despite her technical superiority, we mean that the blows we deliver through annihilation and attrition, apart from inflicting losses, will eventually shake the morale of the enemy army whose weapons are not in the hands of politically conscious soldiers. With us, on the contrary, officers and men are at one on the political aim of the War of Resistance. This gives us the foundation for political work among all the anti-Japanese forces. A proper measure of democracy should be put into effect in the army, chiefly by abolishing the feudal practice of bullying and beating and by having officers and men share weal and woe. Once this is done, unity will be achieved between officers and men, the combat effectiveness of the

army will be greatly increased, and there will be no doubt of our ability to sustain the long, cruel war.

114. The richest source of power to wage war lies in the masses of the people. It is mainly because of the unorganized state of the Chinese masses that Japan dares to bully us. When this defect is remedied, then the Japanese aggressor, like a mad bull crashing into a ring of flames, will be surrounded by hundreds of millions of our people standing upright, the mere sound of their voices will strike terror into him, and he will be burned to death. China's armies must have an uninterrupted flow of reinforcements, and the abuses of press-ganging and of buying substitutes,[33] which now exist at the lower levels, must immediately be banned and replaced by widespread and enthusiastic political mobilization, which will make it easy to enlist millions of men. We now have great difficulties in raising money for the war, but once the people are mobilized, finances too will cease to be a problem. Why should a country as large and populous as China suffer from lack of funds? The army must become one with the people so that they see it as their own army. Such an army will be invincible, and an imperialist power like Japan will be no match for it.

115. Many people think that it is wrong methods that make for strained relations between officers and men and between the army and the people, but I always tell them that it is a question of basic attitude (or basic principle), of having respect for the soldiers and the people. It is from this attitude that the various policies, methods and forms ensue. If we depart from this attitude, then the policies, methods and forms will certainly be wrong, and the relations between officers and men and between the army and the people are bound to be unsatisfactory. Our three major principles for the army's political work are, first, unity between officers and men; second, unity between the army and the people; and third, the

disintegration of the enemy forces. To apply these principles effectively, we must start with this basic attitude of respect for the soldiers and the people, and of respect for the human dignity of prisoners of war once they have laid down their arms. Those who take all this as a technical matter and not one of basic attitude are indeed wrong, and they should correct their view.

116. At this moment when the defense of Wuhan and other places has become urgent, it is a task of the utmost importance to arouse the initiative and enthusiasm of the whole army and the whole people to the full in support of the war. There is no doubt that the task of defending Wuhan and other places must be seriously posed and seriously performed. But whether we can be certain of holding them depends not on our subjective desires but on concrete conditions. Among the most important of these conditions is the political mobilization of the whole army and people for the struggle. If a strenuous effort is not made to secure all the necessary conditions, indeed even if one of these conditions is missing, disasters like the loss of Nanking and other places are bound to be repeated. China will have her Madrids in places where the conditions are present. So far China has not had a Madrid, and from now on we should work hard to create several, but it all depends on the conditions. The most fundamental of these is extensive political mobilization of the whole army and people.

117. In all our work we must persevere in the Anti-Japanese National United Front as the general policy. For only with this policy can we persevere in the War of Resistance and in protracted warfare, bring about a widespread and profound improvement in the relations between officers and men and between the army and the people, arouse to the full the initiative and enthusiasm of the entire army and the entire people in the fight for the defense of all the territory still in our

hands and for the recovery of what we have lost, and so win final victory.

118. This question of the political mobilization of the army and the people is indeed of the greatest importance. We have dwelt on it at the risk of repetition precisely because victory is impossible without it. There are, of course, many other conditions indispensable to victory, but political mobilization is the most fundamental. The Anti-Japanese National United Front is a united front of the whole army and the whole people, it is certainly not a united front merely of the headquarters and members of a few political parties; our basic objective in initiating the Anti-Japanese National United Front is to mobilize the whole army and the whole people to participate in it.

# CONCLUSIONS

119. What are our conclusions? They are:

"Under what conditions do you think China can defeat and destroy the forces of Japan?" "Three conditions are required: first, the establishment of an anti-Japanese united front in China; second, the formation of an international anti-Japanese united front; third, the rise of the revolutionary movement of the people in Japan and the Japanese colonies. From the standpoint of the Chinese people, the unity of the people of China is the most important of the three conditions."

"How long do you think such a war would last?" "That depends on the strength of China's anti-Japanese united front and many other conditioning factors involving China and Japan."

"If these conditions are not realized quickly, the war will be prolonged. But in the end, just the same, Japan will certainly be defeated and China will certainly be victorious. Only the sacrifices will be great and there will be a very painful period."

"Our strategy should be to employ our main forces to operate over an extended and fluid front. To achieve success, the Chinese troops must conduct their warfare with a high degree of mobility on extensive battlefields."

"Besides employing trained armies to carry on mobile warfare, we must organize great numbers of guerrilla units among the peasants."

"In the course of the war, China will be able to . . . reinforce the equipment of her troops gradually. Therefore China will be able to conduct positional warfare in the latter period of the war and make positional attacks on the Japanese-occupied areas. Thus Japan's economy will crack under the strain of China's long resistance and the morale of the Japanese forces will break under the trial of innumerable battles. On the Chinese side, however, the growing latent power of resistance will be constantly brought into play and large numbers of revolutionary people will be pouring into the front lines to fight for their freedom. The combination of all these and other factors will enable us to make the final and decisive attacks on the fortifications and bases in the Japanese occupied areas and drive the Japanese forces of aggression out of China." (From an interview with Edgar Snow in July 1936.)

"Thus a new stage has opened in China's political situation. . . . In the present stage the central task is to mobilize all the nation's forces for victory in the War of Resistance."

"The key to victory in the war now lies in developing the resistance that has already begun into a war of total resistance by the whole nation. Only through such a war of total resistance can final victory be won."

"The existence of serious weaknesses in the War of Resistance may lead to setbacks, retreats, internal splits, betrayals, temporary and partial compromises and other such reverses. Therefore it should be realized that the war will be arduous and protracted. But we are confident that, through the efforts of our Party and the whole people, the resistance already started will sweep aside all obstacles and continue to advance and develop." ("Resolution on the Present Situation and the Tasks of the Party", adopted by the Central Committee of the Communist Party of China, August 1937.)

These are our conclusions. In the eyes of the subjugationists the enemy are supermen and we Chinese are worthless, while in the eyes of the theorists of quick victory we Chinese are supermen and the enemy are worthless. Both are wrong. We take a different view; the War of Resistance against Japan is a protracted war, and the final victory will be China's. These are our conclusions.

120. My lectures end here. The great War of Resistance against Japan is unfolding, and many people are hoping for a summary of experience to facilitate the winning of complete victory. What I have discussed is simply the general experience of the past ten months, and it may perhaps serve as a kind of summary. The problem of protracted war deserves wide attention and discussion; what I have given is only an outline, which I hope you will examine and discuss, amend and amplify.

## NOTES

[1] This theory of national subjugation was the view held by the Kuomintang. The Kuomintang was unwilling to resist Japan and fought Japan only under compulsion. After the Lukouchiao Incident (July 7. 1937), the Chiang Kai-shek clique reluctantly took part in the War of Resistance, while the Wang Ching-wei clique became the representatives of the theory of national subjugation, was ready to capitulate to Japan and in fact subsequently did so. However, the idea of national subjugation not only existed in the Kuomintang, but also affected certain sections of the middle strata of society and even certain backward elements among the laboring people. As the corrupt and impotent Kuomintang government lost one battle after another and the Japanese troops advanced unchecked to the vicinity of Wuhan in the first year of the War of Resistance, some backward people became profoundly pessimistic.

[2] These views were to be found within the Communist Party. During the first six months of the War of Resistance, there was a tendency to take the enemy lightly among some members of the Party, who held the view that Japan could be defeated at a single blow. It was not that they felt our own forces to be so strong, since they well knew that the troops and the organized people's forces led by the Communist Party were still small, but that the Kuomintang had begun to resist Japan. In their opinion, the Kuomintang was quite powerful, and, in co-ordination with the Communist Party, could deal Japan telling blows. They made this erroneous appraisal because they saw only one aspect of the Kuomintang, that it was resisting Japan, but overlooked the other aspect, that it was reactionary and corrupt.

[3] Such was the view of Chiang Kai-shek and company. Though they were compelled to resist Japan, Chiang Kai-shek and the Kuomintang pinned their hopes solely on prompt foreign aid and had no confidence in their own strength, much less in the strength of the people.

[4] Taierhchuang is a town in southern Shantung where the Chinese army fought a battle in March 1938 against the Japanese invaders. By pitting 400,000 men against Japan's 70,000 to 80,000, the Chinese army defeated the Japanese.

[5] This view was put forward in an editorial in the Ta Kung Pao, then the organ of the Political Science Group in the Kuomintang. Indulging in wishful thinking, this clique hoped that a few more victories of the Taierhchuang type would stop Japan's advance and that there would be no need to mobilize the people for a protracted war, which would threaten the security of its own class. This wishful thinking then pervaded the Kuomintang as a whole.

[6] For many decades, beginning with the end of the 18th century, Britain exported an increasing quantity of opium to China. This traffic not only subjected the Chinese people to drugging but also plundered China of her silver. It aroused fierce opposition in China. In 1840, under the pretext of safeguarding its trade with China, Britain launched armed aggression against her. The Chinese troops led by Lin Tse-hsu put up resistance, and the people in Canton spontaneously organized the "Quell-the British Corps", which dealt serious blows to the British forces of aggression. In 1842, however, the corrupt Ching regime signed the Treaty of Ninking with Britain. This treaty provided for the payment of indemnities and the cession of Hong Kong to Britain, and stipulated that Shanghai, Foochow, Amoy, Ningpo and Canton were to be opened to British trade and that tariff rates for British goods

imported into China were to be jointly fixed by China and Britain.

[7] The Taiping Revolution, or the Movement of the Taiping Heavenly Kingdom, was the mid-19th century revolutionary peasant movement against the feudal rule and national oppression of the Ching Dynasty. In Janualy 1851 Hung Hsiu-chuan, Yang Hsiu-ching and other leaders launched an uprising in Chintien Village in Kueiping County, Kwangsi Province, and proclaimed the founding of the Taiping Heavenly Kingdom. Proceeding northward from Kwangsi, their peasant army at tacked and occupied Hunan and Hupeh in 1852. In 1853 it marched through Kiangsi and Anhwei and captured Nanking. A section of the force then continued the drive north and pushed on to the vicinity of Tientsin. However the Taiping army failed to build stable base areas in the places it occupied; moreover, after establishing its capital in Nanking, its leading group committed many political and military errors. Therefore it was unable to withstand the combined onslaughts of the counter revolutionary forces of the Ching government and the British, U.S. and French aggressors, and was finally defeated in 1864.

[8] The Reform Movement of 1898, whose leading spirits were Kang Yu-wei, Liang Chi-chao and Tan Szu-tung represented the interests of the liberal bourgeoisie and the enlightened landlords. The movement was favored and supported by Emperor Kuang Hsu, but had no mass basis. Yuan Shih-kai, who had an army behind him, betrayed the reformers to Empress Dowager Tzu Hsi, the leader of the die-hards, who seized power again and had Emperor Kuang Hsu imprisoned and Tan Szu-tung and five others beheaded. Thus the movement ended in tragic defeat.

[9] The Revolution of 1911 was the bourgeois revolution which overthrew the autocratic regime of the Ching Dynasty. On October 10 of that year, a section of the Ching Dynasty's New Army who were under revolutionary influence staged an uprising in Wuchang, Hupeh Province. The existing bourgeois and petty-bourgeois revolutionary societies and the broad masses of the workers, peasants and soldiers responded enthusiastically, and very soon the rule of the Ching Dynasty crumbled. In January 1912, the Provisional Government of the Republic of China was set up in Nanking, with Sun Yat-sen as the Provisional President. Thus China's feudal monarchic system which had lasted for more than two thousand years was brought to an end. The idea of a democratic republic had entered deep in the hearts of the people. But the bourgeoisie which led the revolution was strongly conciliationist in nature. It did not mobilize the peasant masses on an extensive scale to crush the feudal rule of the landlord class in the countryside, but instead handed state power over to the Northern warlord Yuan Shih-kai under imperialist and feudal pressure. As a result, the revolution ended in defeat.

[10] The Northern Expedition was the punitive war against the Northern war lords launched by the revolutionary army which marched north from Kwangtung Province in May-July 1926. The Northern Expeditionary Army, with the Communist Party of China taking part in its leadership and under the Party's influence (the political work in the army was at that time mostly under the charge of Communist Party members), gained the warm support of the broad masses of workers and peasants. In the second half of 1926 and the first half of 1927 it occupied most of the provinces along the Yangtse and Yellow Rivers and defeated the Northern warlords. In April 1927 this revolutionary war failed as a result of betrayal by the reactionary clique under Chiang Kai-shek within the revolutionary army.

[11] On January 16, 1938, the Japanese cabinet declared in a policy statement that Japan would subjugate China by force. At the same time it tried by threats and blandishments to make the Kuomintang government capitulate, declaring that if the Kuomintang government "continued to plan resistance", the Japanese government would foster a new puppet regime in China and no longer accept the Kuomintang as "the other party" in negotiations.

[12] The capitalists referred to here are chiefly those of the United States.

[13] By "their governments" Comrade Mao Zedong is here referring to the governments of the imperialist countries -- Britain, the United States and France.

[14] Comrade Mao Zedong's prediction that there would be an upswing in China during the stage of stalemate in the War of Resistance against Japan was completely confirmed in the case of the Liberated Areas under the leadership of the Chinese Communist Party. But there was actually a decline instead of an upswing in the Kuomintang areas, because the ruling clique headed by Chiang Kai-shek was passive in resisting Japan and active in opposing the Communist Party and the people. This roused opposition among the broad masses of the people and raised their political consciousness.

[15] According to the theory that "weapons decide everything", China which was inferior to Japan in regard to arms was bound to be defeated in the war. This view was current among all the leaders of the Kuomintang reaction, Chiang Kai-shek included.

[16] See "Problems of Strategy in Guerrilla War Against Japan", Note 9, p. 112 of this volume.

[17] Sun Wu-kung is the monkey king in the Chinese novel Hsi Yu Chi (Pilgrimage to thc West ), written in the 16th century. He could cover 108,000 li by turning a somersault. Yet once in the palm of the Buddha, he could not escape from it, however many somersaults he turned. With a flick of his palm Buddha transformed his fingers into the five-peak Mountain of Five Elements, and buried Sun Wu-kung.

[18] "Fascism is unbridled chauvinism and predatory war," said Comrade Georgi Dimitrov in his report to the Seventh World Congress of the Communist International in August 1935, entitled "The Fascist Offensive and the Tasks of the Communist International" (see Selected Articles and Speeches, Eng. ed., Lawrence & Wishart, London, 1951, p. 44). In July 1937, Comrade Dimitrov published an article entitled Fascism Is War.

[19] V. I. Lenin, Socialism and War, Eng. ed., FLPH, Moscow, 1950, p. 19.

[20] Sun Tzu, Chapter 3, "The Strategy of Attack".

[21] Chengpu, situated in. the southwest of the present Chuancheng County in Shantung Province, was the scene of a great battle between the states of Tsin and Chu in 632 B.C. At the beginning of the battle the Chu troops got the upper hand. The Tsin troops, after making a retreat of 90 li, chose the right and left flanks of the Chu troops, their weak spots, and inflicted heavy defeats on them.

[22] The ancient town of Chengkao, in the northwest of the present Chengkao County, Honan Province, was of great

military importance. It was the scene of battles fought in 203 B.C. between Liu Pang, King of Han, and Hsiang Yu, King of Chu. At first Hsiang Yu captured Hsingyang and Chengkao and Liu Pang's troops were almost routed. Liu Pang waited until the opportune moment when Hsiang Yu's troops were in midstream crossing the Szeshui River, and then crushed them and recaptured Chengkao.

[23] In 204 B.C., Han Hsin, a general of the state of Han, led his men in a big battle with Chao Hsieh at Chinghsing. Chao Hsieh's army, said to be 200,000 strong, was several times that of Han. Deploying his troops with their backs to a river, Han Hsin led them in valiant combat, and at the same time dispatched some units to attack and occupy the enemy's weakly garrisoned rear. Caught in a pincer, Chao Hsieh's troops were utterly defeated.

[24] The ancient town of Kunyang, in the north of the present Yehhsien County, Honan Province, was the place where Liu Hsiu, founder of the Eastern Han Dynasty, defeated the troops of Wang Mang, Emperor of the Hsin Dynasty, in A.D. 23. There was a huge numerical disparity between the two sides, Liu Hsiu's forces totalling 8,000 to 9,000 men as against Wang Mang's 400,000. But taking advantage of the negligence of Wang Mang's generals, Wang Hsun and Wang Yi, who underestimated the enemy, Liu Hsiu with only three thousand picked troops put Wang Mang's main forces to rout. He followed up this victory by crushing the rest of the enemy troops.

[25] Kuantu was in the northeast of the present Chungmou County, Honan Province, and the scene of the battle between the armies of Tsao Tsao and Yuan Shao in A.D.

200. Yuan Shao had an army of 100,000, while Tsao Tsao had only a meager force and was short of supplies. Taking advantage of the lack of vigilance on the part of Yuan Shao's troops, who belittled the enemy, Tsao Tsao dispatched his light-footed soldiers to spring a surprise attack on them and set their supplies on fire. Yuan Shao's army was thrown into confusion and its main force wiped out.

[26] The sute of Wu was ruled by Sun Chuan, and the sute of Wei by Tsao Tsao. Chihpi is situated on the south bank of the Yangtse River, to the northeast of Chiayu, Hupeh Province. In A.D. 208 Tsao Tsao led an army of over 500,000 men, which he proclaimed to be 800,000 strong, to launch an attack on Sun Chuan. The latter, in alliance with Tsao Tsao's antagonist Liu Pei, mustered a force of 30,000. Knowing that Tsao Tsao's army was plagued by epidemics and was unaccustomed to action afloat, the allied forces of Sun Chuan and Liu Pei set fire to Tsao Tsao's fleet and crushed his army.

[27] Yiling, to the east of the present Ichang, Hupeh Province, was the place where Lu Sun, a general of the sute of Wu, defeated the army of Liu Pei, ruler of Shu, in A.D. 222. Liu Pei's troops scored successive victories at the beginning of the war and penetrated five or six hundred li into the territory of Wu as far as Yiling. Lu Sun, who was defending Yiling, avoided battle for over seven months until Liu Pei "was at his wits' end and his troops were exhausted and demoralized". Then he crushed Liu Pei's troops by taking advantage of a favorable wind to set fire to their tents.

[28] Hsieh Hsuan, a general of Eastern Tsin Dynasty, defeated Fu Chien, ruler of the state of Chin, in A.D. 383 at the Feishui River in Anhwei Province. Fu Chien had an infantry force of more than 600,000, a cavalry force of 270,000 and a guards corps of more than 30,000, while the land and river

forces of Eastern Tsin numbered only 80,000. When the armies lined up on opposite banks of the Feishui River, Hsieh Hsuan, taking advantage of the overconfidence and conceit of the enemy troops, requested Fu Chien to move his troops back so as to leave room for the Eastern Tsin troops to cross the river and fight it out. Fu Chien complied, but when he ordered withdrawal, his troops got into a panic and could not be stopped. Seizing the opportunity, the Eastern Tsin troops crossed the river, launched an offensive and crushed the enemy.

[29] In A.D. 383, Fu Chien, the ruler of the state of Chin, belittled the forces of Tsin and attacked them. The Tsin troops defeated the enemy's advance units at Lochien, Shouyang County, Anhwei Province, and pushed forward by land and water. Ascending the city wall of Shouyang, Fu Chien observed the excellent alignment of the Tsin troops and, mistaking the woods and bushes on Mount Pakung for enemy soldiers, was frightened by the enemy's apparent strength.

[30] Comrade Mao Zedong is here referring to the fact that Chiang Kai-shek and Wang Ching-wei, having betrayed the first national democratic united front of the Kuomintang and the Communist Party in 1927, launched a ten-year war against the people, and thus made it impossible for the Chinese people to be organized on a large scale. For this the Kuomintang reactionaries headed by Chiang Kai-shek must be held responsible.

[31] Duke Hsiang of Sung ruled in the Spring and Autumn Era. In 638 B.C., the state of Sung fought with the powerful state of Chu. The Sung forces were already deployed in battle positions when the Chu troops were crossing the river. One of the Sung officers suggested that, as the Chu troops were numerically stronger, this was the moment for attack. But the

Duke said, "No, a gentleman should never attack one who is unprepared." When the Chu troops had crossed the river but had not yet completed their battle alignment, the officer again proposed an immediate attack, and once again the Duke said, "No, a gentleman should never attack an army which has not yet completed its battle alignment." The Duke gave the order for attack only after the Chu troops were fully prepared. As a result, the Sung troops met with a disastrous defeat and the Duke himself was wounded.

[32] Han Fu-chu, a Kuomintang warlord, was for several years governor of Shantung. When the Japanese invaders thrust southward to Shantung along the Tientsin-pukow Railway after occupying Peiping and Tientsin in 1937, Han Fu-chu fled all the way from Shantung to Honan without fighting a single battle.

[33] The Kuomintang expanded its army by press-ganging. Its military and police seized people everywhere, roping them up and treating them like convicts. Those who had money would bribe the Kuomintang officials or pay for substitutes.

CPSIA information can be obtained at www.ICGtesting.com
Printed in the USA
LVOW061012051012

301619LV00001B/174/P